TYPEPLAY

NIPPAN

Steven Heller & Gail Anderson

Designed by
Alexander Isley
Design

Library Of Congress Cataloging–in–Publication Data

Heller, Steven
Typeplay/by Steven Heller & Gail Anderson
p.   cm.
Includes index.
ISBN 3-910052-51-7
1. Printing—United States.   2. Type and type-founding—United States.   3. Graphic Arts—United States
I. Anderson, Gail, 1962-.   II. Title
Z208.H39 1994   94-5872
686.2'24--dc20   CIP
First published in Germany by:
NIPPAN
Nippon Shuppan Hanbai
Deutschland GmbH; Krefelder Str. 85; D-40549 Düsseldorf
Telephone: (0211) 5048089 Fax: (0211) 5049326
Color separation by Fine Arts Repro House Co.,Ltd., H.K.
Printing and binding by Toppan Printing Co.(H.K.) Ltd. Hong Kong.

Printed in Hong Kong

10 9 8 7 6 5 4 3 2

To Paul Rand

Intense as any thriller, lusty as any romance, and wanton as any book on this subject can be, this is a book about type and lettering, and wanton is not an overstatement. Today there is definitely wanton disregard for the rules of typography. Yet one's wantonness is another's freedom. One's rules are another's license. So let's say that this is a book about passion; a passionate, often smoldering love affair between graphic designers and letterforms, in parts a veritable Kama Sutra of typography revealing many kinds of typographic love—from the sensual hot metal kiss to the orgasmic distortion of digital fonts.

Other than type there are few issues that so completely consume the graphic designer. Illustration is fun, layout is challenging, but typography is the sine qua non of all graphic design endeavor. Societies and clubs celebrate it, conferences debate it, and publications dissect it. Like politics and art, the world of typography has its zealots on both the right and left.

And although type itself is often neutral few designers are neutral about typographic issues, as this sampling of quotations attests:

"Now we have personal computers...that allows you to distort and manipulate type at your whim without any knowledge of type..." railed Massimo Vignelli in *Print* magazine in 1992. "Now they've got a tool that gives them license to kill. This is the new level of visual pollution."

"...[W]e are not interested in a passive and servile relationship to communication, but [one] that is rigorously engaging," stated Jeffery Keedy in *Emigre* #21.

"As a typographer, you are the servant of the author..." cautioned Rauri McLean in *Typography* (1988), "Your job is to help the author to reach his public. You are not making works of art of your own; you are transmitting, with as much skill...the words of someone else."

"All language is personal and that, to me, justifies very personal typefaces," argued Neville Brody in *Eye* magazine in 1992.

"Personal typography is defective typography," exhorted Jan Tschicold in *The Form of the Book* in 1975.

Vociferous debates over type's form and function like this have raged for decades among typographers. Going back further in time type has also symbolized ideology and dogma. In the fifteenth century the distinction between capitals and uncials, for example, mirrored the separation of social classes, as well as being a revolutionary alteration of the written "voice." During the 1930s, in the early years of the Nazi regime, sans serif letters were condemned as anti-German—"a Jewish invention," asserted the Nazi propaganda minister Dr. Joseph Goebbels—and were temporarily replaced by the awkward, though decidedly Germanic, spiky Fraktur. Type should be viewed as more than a bridge between writing and print or a manifestation of language: it is a cultural signpost by which a variety of social phenomena can be examined.

Type is one of the cornerstones of civilization. Aesthetics that developed during the early Renaissance, when classical Greek and Roman culture (art and architecture) was reappreciated and revived, directly influenced the design of letterforms and the archetypes of beauty. The standards applied to typographic balance and harmony echoed those of the major arts, and extended to the applied arts, too. Classical typefaces represented the highest ideals of Western culture. As a humanist art, typography during the Renaissance was as important as painting and sculpture. The masters were among the most progressive artisans of the day for they developed forms that extended the boundaries of communications. In a preliterate world they brought the written word to life by providing structure. By giving it form—indeed nuance—they preserved the word in a manner that could be appreciated centuries later.

Types that were developed during the sixteenth and seventeenth centuries continue to be the models for most typographic endeavor today. Whether the method is traditional or progressive, typography is based, either through adherence or rejection, on the basic principles developed during this critical time. For some designers the traditional or classical approach is as sacrosanct as any religious doctrine, and as zealously preserved. "Type is rigid and implacable," wrote Frederick W. Goudy in *Typologia* in 1921. With others the past is not an end in

itself but the foundation upon which to build new traditions. "We've had five hundred years of moveable type now we have mutable type," concedes Matthew Carter in *Fine Print on Type* (1990). Rebellion is built upon this foundation, too. Those who believe that the classical approach represents archaic standards—better entombed than perpetuated—also hold that traditional typography is the embodiment of oppressive formality. "Of all the arts and crafts, none more lives in the dirty tepid bath water of the past than does typography," declared British designer Phil Baines in *Typographic Magazine* (1991) who would agree that type, like twentieth-century art, has become an expressionistic endeavor. Owing to its solemn rationality classicism is viewed by today's practitioners as expressionism's apotheosis.

And yet the Modern movement of the 1920s, though a rebellious one, actually reconciled contemporary and classical values by rejecting timeworn verities in favor of timeless utility. Styleless functionalism was the hallmark of Bauhaus typography, although it eventually evolved into a style. The real tension in typography has for decades existed between rationalism and expressionism, or rather objective versus subjective aesthetics. Jan Tschicold, who having helped codify the objectivist New Typography in 1925 eventually returned to traditional methods, wrote in *The Form of the Book:* "The aim of typography must not be expression, least of all self-expression.... In a masterpiece of typography, the artist's signature has been eliminated. What some may praise as personal styles are in reality small and empty peculiarities, frequently damaging, that masquerade as innovations." Yet despite this admonition, Tschicold was the chief proselytizer for a

movement that attacked the visual redundancy that was the by-product of traditionalism. His doctrine of asymmetry literally stood type on its ear in an effort to garner greater attention. His predilection for sans serif as opposed to serif faces was based on what he and other Modernists believed were objective truths. Yet critics accused them of perpetrating myths to support their assertions of legibility. Perhaps the contemporary Dutch typographer Gerard Unger is correct when in *Emigre #23* he argued, "Tschicold's preference for sans serifs, and his opinion that they...were more legible than typefaces with serifs, were based upon emotional considerations."

Tschicold and other seminal Modern typographers developed the rules of rationalism that were fervently adopted in the postwar era by a new generation of Moderns in Switzerland, Germany, and America that rallied under the banner *Neue Grafik* or New Graphics. They pushed objectivity and rationalism to a precipice where it balanced between being progressive and progressively redundant. In part, this approach developed as a predictable reaction to the fundamentally crass commercial art in which typographic "expression" was characterized by letters frozen in icicles, consumed in flames, and carved with motion-lines to represent, respectively, cold, heat, and speed. Modern typographic principles were developed to prevent the callous abuse of both au courant and passé typefaces and letters. But under the hard rules established to prevent various aesthetic indiscretions, other crimes and misdemeanors were committed. The worst of which was that graphic design, regardless of subject or context, began to look the same. "Oh, Tschicold...under the disguise of neutrality and readability..., your

9

imitators conquered the world," reads the purple prose of Frank Heine in *Emigre #23.* "See what they did to mankind? They hushed it with boredom until its discernment completely slacked. Your imitators suffocated the world with their mediocrity, coated her with global conformity."

It was this trend toward Modern redundancy that led to mediocrity and fostered another movement of aesthetic values that was neither traditional nor Modern, but eclectic. Eclecticism was based on revivals of old-fashioned popular graphic styles such as Victorian, Art Nouveau, and Art Deco. In a prefiguration of Post-Modernism, eclecticism rejected both cold objectivity and elegant classicism in favor of what in today's argot is called the vernacular, the indigenous language of commercial art. The American Moderns, including Paul Rand, Alvin Lustig, and Lester Beall, sought to distinguish themselves from the majority of anonymous commercial artists by taking on the new (and somewhat heroic) titles of "designer for industry" and "graphic designer," and adopted many of the principles of fine Modern art, which underscored a wished for transcendency of the cultural significance of Modern design. The eclecticists, on the other hand, including Push Pin Studios and Herb Lubalin, derived their styles (and strength) from the legacy of *commercial* art, borrowing and appropriating it as personal style.

For the eclecticists universality was rejected in favor of individualism. The Moderns sought a common language, the eclecticists strived for uncommon solutions. The Moderns rejected supercilious ornamentation, the eclecticists enthusiastically embraced it, not in a nostalgic sense but to enhance presentation of the message by warming and personalizing it. Their work was influenced by the past but was decidedly contemporary. The Moderns believed that design should be "of its time"; the eclecticists decided that their times demanded variety, and that revived forms had as much validity as new ones. Moreover, since new phototypesetting technologies were making it possible to achieve unprecedented results, there was an increased potential for typographic expression using both new and old typefaces.

Herb Lubalin, a devout typophile, and in the 1960s a master of commercial typographic "experimentation," argued for change in this way in *Typography U.S.A.* (1959): "We've been conditioned to read the way Gutenberg set his type, and for 500 years people have been reading widely-spaced words on horizontal lines Gutenberg spaced far apart....We read words, not characters, and pushing letters closer or tightening space between lines doesn't destroy legibility; it merely changes reading habits." Lubalin built upon the ideas of earlier twentieth-century type/image-makers, such as Kurt Schwitters and Lazar El Lizzitsky, and blurred the distinction between type and image. In fact, Lubalin's approach was very much of its time given his understanding of the effect of new technologies on contemporary perception. In 1959 Lubalin argued before an assembly of typographers that television had begun to have an impact on the way that type was read, and likened this kineticism to the speed in which type shoots by on advertising on the sides of buses. He reasoned that in this environment smashing letterforms together (which was Lubalin's trademark) and including images in a rebus-like manner made type easier to decipher.

In the late 1940s a pioneer of American typography, Bradbury Thompson, edited and designed the influential periodical *Westvaco Inspirations* in which he encouraged designers to occasionally release type from its moorings and play with it as if it were a toy. His idea, inspired by the Futurists, Dadaists and Surrealists of the 1920s, was that smart typographic puns could be made from letterforms which would enhance reading by providing an additional level of meaning. Thompson made puns with letterforms that released specific sounds, not unlike the onomatopoeic type poems of the Italian Futurists. A decade or so later Herb Lubalin took the idea even further by combining photographs and drawings with expressive letters that underscored or amplified the meaning of a headline. This was serious typeplay—and Lubalin was a fiddler par excellence. Yet his mission was not to toy with or confuse the reader but to promote clarity. "Typography must be clear communication in its most vivid form," warned Bauhaus type master Laszlo Moholy-Nagy. And although Lubalin's display compositions were not of the style that Moholy was promoting, they were indeed vivid, if at times risqué. Despite the liberties that Lubalin routinely took with typography his work was not difficult to decipher. While he tampered with the form, he stayed loyal to the purpose of type which meant that on some level it must be legible.

Legibility, as opposed to quality, is at the heart of the arguments, pro and con, about typeplay and experimentation. "Legibility is a dangerous—and interesting—word," wrote the English type historian Rauri McLean in *Typography* (1988). "It is dangerous because it is so often used as if it had a definitive or absolute meaning. Which it does not have. It is a personal word, neither scientific nor precise."

Therefore, what is illegible to one can be legible to another, depending on one's specific orientation. In the late 1960s, at the same time that Lubalin was tweaking typographic conventions, a younger generation of American *graphistes*, the Psychedelic poster artists, were violently upsetting typographic propriety, and like some of the mind-enhancing drugs that they consumed their unvarnished type compositions were testing the limits of perception. Victor Moscoso, a leading proponent, turned many canonical rules of legibility and clarity upside down. He used vibrating colors and slab serif types packed tightly together in compositions that were as difficult to read as possible. Yet they were not illegible. "The common wisdom that a passerby had to absorb a poster in ten seconds flat was as ridiculous as it was arbitrary; I wanted them to spend five, ten, even fifteen minutes with it," explained Moscoso years later. And why not? The decree that posters had to be simplistic was imposed by advertising experts who believed that in the highly competitive commercial marketplace simplicity provided the competing edge. Moscoso reasoned that the "consumers" of San Francisco rock and roll were not like the typical dashing commuter and could therefore afford the time to absorb and decipher the poster's message. The fact that it was a kind of game that the reader could understand by being a member of the "tribe" made it additionally appealing. Hence, what appeared illegible to the outsider was crystal clear to the cognoscenti.

"Legibility, in practice, amounts simply to what one is accustomed to," wrote Eric Gill in *An Essay on Typography* (1934). And what one was accustomed to in the late 1960s and early 1970s was the loosening of the verbal and visual language. If typography is, as Jan Tschicold once observed, "a servant and nothing more," then it stood to reason that typography would have to reflect the emerging cultural revolutions either in substance or style. In the early seventies, with the demise of psychedelia, graphic design entered a period of uncertain transition from Modern to Post-Modern. As Herb Lubalin had predicted over a decade before, television and video were having a profound impact on perception, and gradually the computer was also beginning to suggest new typographic directions, if only tangentially at first. These factors partly contributed to the inevitable schism of old and new that had its first major eruption in Basel, Switzerland, the home of Neue Grafik and the International Style of rational typography. "Pure typography is not the only way to convey a message," said Wolfgang Weingart, the major proponent and teacher of the new New Typography. "It's value and potential depends directly on its ambiguity."

As a onetime student of the rigid, and anything but ambiguous, Swiss style, Weingart was poised to break the rules of simplicity and clarity. While continuing to use the fundamental elements of Swiss typography—Univers, Helvetica, and Akidenz Grotesk typefaces—he began to deconstruct typographic composition. Complex layers of boldface, italic, and roman letterforms, often set against ambiguous or "noisy" backgrounds, sometimes in what appeared to be an approximation of video display screens, became the paradigm for a new typographic direction and style. In the fast-paced information age, it was reasoned that traditional reading habits—specifically regarding ephemeral materials such as posters, magazines, and newspapers—would eventually be altered by technology, as they have been throughout the history of mass communications. Contemporary typography, the servant of language, needed to include many entry (and exit) points designed for the increasingly more harried reader. Through highlighted and underscored words and phrases, through intersecting ideas and thoughts, this new typography allowed the reader to choose points of interest, much in the way pull-quotes or blurbs had been used in magazines and newspapers. While on the surface this looked like type as texture—ornament, not words—the new method was very much about accentuating the word and stimulating comprehension through the introduction of "type bites." The new Swiss typography began as a youthful rejection of Modern verities yet its multilayered aesthetic eventually became a metaphor for the information and computer ages and was adopted outside the confines of the hothouse. In so doing it posed a threat to the established Modern order, and was dubbed ugly by those whose fundamental beliefs in typographic objectivity were challenged.

"As typography addresses everyone, it leaves no room for revolutionary change," wrote Jan Tschicold in *Print* magazine (1959) in words that spoke for traditionalists and orthodox Moderns alike. "We cannot even fundamentally change one single letterform without destroying the typeset representation of our language and render it useless." But this sermon ignores the fact that global politics and culture were radically altered after World War II, indeed language itself had profoundly changed over that time, and type as its servant also had to undergo periodic overhauls. By the 1980s the social as well as technological environment had been so profoundly changed that all segments of the culture demanded reevaluation. "Lately we've moved into an era of more cultural fragmentation and ethnic celebration...," stated Katherine McCoy in *Emigre* #19, "You have to be a chameleon to shape your message to the audience so that you can resonate with that audience." McCoy, who codirects the graduate design program at Cranbrook Academy of Art, is a proponent of Post-Modern—or what some call deconstructive—typography, a logical evolutionary offshoot of the Swiss grid-busting school, and the most radically experimental manifestations of contemporary American typeplay. What began in Switzerland as a mildly expressive use of letterforms spread to other parts of Europe (notably Holland) and the United States where in academies like Cranbrook, Rhode Island School of Design, and California Institute of the Arts expressionism became an end in itself. Wed to certain avant-garde linguistic theories and influenced by mass media, "decon" or "PM" typography was not only concerned with busting Modern strictures, but developing codes that would "resonate" with various audiences by drawing them in through multiple levels of visual/verbal data, not unlike computer/video games that push the player through increasingly complex levels of stimuli.

"What is new about Cranbrook's direction is the infusion of meaning into the production of a plethora of objects and graphics that have become mundane and boring," wrote industrial designer Niels Diffrient in *The New Cranbrook Design Discourse* (1990). "It can perhaps be argued that Modernism...also had meaning. And indeed it did, but the meaning most often

was in expressing the materials, function, and process rather than the subtleties of human interaction. This often resulting in a kind of dry neatness, devoid of the essential messiness and ambiguity of the human condition." In contrast to the words "neutrality" and "simplicity," which were mantras of the Moderns, "ambiguity" and "complexity" underscore a contemporary, chaotic ethic and aesthetic and reflect what designers today believe represents the harsh realities of life. "Many people feel it's their role in life to destroy all ambiguity," stated Jeffery Keedy in *Emigre* #16. "I think that ambiguity is life itself and it's what makes life interesting. We too often assume that people are so stupid that they can't deal with ambiguity. I think people live for ambiguity and complexity."

As Modernism was a utopian aesthetic and ethical reaction to the debauched bourgeois societies of pre– and post–World War I Europe, and was initially viewed with contempt by the keepers of the bourgeoisie, so is Post-Modernism a response to the archaic and unresponsive strictures and styles that derived from the Moderns. Historically reaction to a previous generation can be either conservative or radical depending on the tenor of the times. That contemporary typography is raucous and anarchic is a logical repudiation of the cool rationalism that marked the immediate past. But it is also a reprise of early Modern (i.e. Futurist and Dadaist principles), which took art to task for being moribund.

The ideal of "art" has recently been imbued in typography, which prior to now was ostensibly practiced as a craft. Not that typography was ever without its artistic underpinnings, for example "Bodoni created typefaces and typography to impress the eye," wrote type historian Allan Haley in

Typographic Milestones (1992), "His designs were studied efforts to be seen as well as to be read..." But certainly the traditionalists agree that typography is, as the British typographer Stanley Morrison once noted, "essentially utilitarian and only accidentally aesthetic." The personal computer has become a canvas on which type has become the equivalent of paint. Digitization has made it possible for the tutored and untutored to play at will, indeed create art with letterforms. Though following the tradition of concrete poetics and letter collages by the early Moderns, their challenge to academic painting does not apply here. Digital type has simply become a new, and by virtue of is ubiquity, an expedient medium for non- or wanna-be designers. For professional designers, taking on the type designer's role is a more hands-on way to deal with the tools of the trade.

Thanks to the Macintosh, typefaces can now be customized and personalized, and this ability has opened the door to both creative excellence and wanton abuse. Thanks to *Emigre* magazine the application of these types and the experiments of young designers are given a sympathetic showcase. "The reason why we are producing so many typefaces at the moment," states Neville Brody in *Eye* magazine, "is to try to break the mystique of typography. In fact, I think in the future everyone will have their own typeface, which is healthy. With computers that respond to handwriting the digital medium will be personalized." But for some this kind of democracy bodes ill. "I think we have to make a distinction between design and art," Massimo Vignelli cautioned in *Print* magazine, "If you are an artist, you can do anything you want. It's perfectly all right. Design serves a different purpose. If in the process of solving a problem you create a problem, obviously, you didn't design."

Vignelli's statement challenges the entire basis of typeplay. He asserts that the design process has a definite beginning, middle, and end, governed by certain absolutes, the purpose of which is to convey information or ideas. In the current design milieu typography has become another vehicle for expression, to be both indulged and seriously considered. The only way to achieve expressionistic satisfaction is, however, through trial and error, with the errors or "problems" being as important to the creative process as the successes. "I try to work intuitively and to provoke an emotional response from the viewer," explained David Carson, art director of *Ray Gun* in *How* magazine (1992). And Carson's playtime on the computer has resulted in a visual language that communicates directly with a specific constituency in the same way that psychedelia did two decades previous, and for that matter, as Jugenstil (Youth Style) did through its unconventional floriated letterforms almost a century ago. Carson experimented with the quirks and limitations of the Macintosh, its layout and type programs, to find out how limiting or delimiting the new technology could be. He quickly found that it had the power to evoke symbolic connections. "Mentally you cut me, allow my pleasures to pour out onto the pages within, visual ecstasy, bridging subconscious, thoughts become reality, piercing type, chiseled into the page, by minds, not hands, grinding the teeth of reality," wrote a *Ray Gun* reader. "Dear Sirs, your magazine is too hard to read..." wrote another.

As Matthew Carter said, "we now have mutable type," and so perhaps we should accept mutable typographic rules. "Gone are the commercial artist's servant role and the Swiss designer's transparent neutrality...," wrote Katherine McCoy in *Design Quarterly* #148. "Forms are appropriated with a critical awareness of their original meaning and contexts. This new work challenges its audience to slow down and read carefully in a world of fast forward and instant replay..." Yet the Modernist repudiation of the new typeplay is not only based on their fervent adherence to what they believe are immutable laws, but the fact that these laws are the foundation on which graphic design has been transformed from a service into a profession. Before the rules existed anarchy reigned, ad hocism prevailed, and professionalism was a joke. Now with these sacrosanct rules being challenged by serious designers with their own cultural imperatives, as well as artistes and wanna-bes with little understanding, the need to find reconciliation is necessary. "There has to be a balance within the overall complexity between the look of the piece and the actual message that is communicated," wrote Nick Bell in *Emigre* #22. "You don't want the readers to be involved purely in the visual treat, because they will ignore the message." It is this attempt at balancing abandon and constraint that is celebrated in *American Typeplay*.

Contemporary typography is not locked into any one system or ideology, but rather serves different functions that demand different approaches. The examples in *American Typeplay* do not narrowly delineate a single movement, trend, or fashion. Deconstructive, vernacular, neoclassical, and other genres are collected here in an effort to suggest the range of contemporary interest in, and of course passion for, type and typography. This is a record of the commonly uncommon, the conventionally unconventional, and the seriously playful approaches that serve various typographic requirements. While this book does not take any ideological stand, it has a philosophical one: Typeplay is endemic to visual communications. It is fueled by imagination, and imagination requires license. In a diverse culture variety should be encouraged, but standards of quality should somehow govern. License is not limitless. For typeplay not to produce monstrous results the question of what is quality should be paramount. Not all experimentation is good. Not all things new have virtue. It is the nature of typeplay that there will be failures, it is the goal of *American Typeplay* to question, and yet celebrate, the successes.

—Steven Heller

Chapter 1

Playing with scale is one of the first games that one learns as a designer. Differences in scale signal differences in attitude, importance, and character. Understanding the relationships between mass is therefore key to producing graphic excitement. In typography the juxtapositioning of large and small letterforms—not just in the conventional sense between capitals and lowercase or large caps and small caps—gives a work a certain monumentality, indeed it provides the illusion of more than two dimensions. If one thinks of typefaces as the building blocks of design, then toying with random shifts in size is not unlike the typical child's play. Big and small is at once the most simple and curiously complex of the type-plays. On the one hand trial and error born of instinct is necessary to achieve a satisfying result. On the other, instinct must be honed by experience (and taste). Collaging elements without some semblance of forethought does not insure interesting work. Determining the right balance between objects, images, and letterforms is what distinguishes the skilled designer from the amateur. Understanding how to manipulate big and small is essential to making playful compositions. For if the ingredients are mismeasured even a little bit—if the relationships are either not harmonious enough or too disharmonious—the resulting design, whether a poster, magazine layout, or book jacket, will be nothing more than a confusing melange of diverse forms. Despite the overarching playful abandon required, for big and small to succeed the designer must possess a keen understanding of the formal qualities of the materials being used.

B
I G
& SMALL

Book Jacket
As Long As Nothing Happens
Nothing Will

Art Director
Krystyna Skalski

Designer
Carin Goldberg

Photographer
Benno Friedman

© *Grove Press* 1990

Book Jacket
Cousins

Designer
Archie Ferguson

Photographer
Michael Horner

© *Alfred A. Knopf* 1992

Magazine Spread
San Francisco Focus

Art Director/Designer
Matthew Drace

Illustrator
Barry Blitt

© *San Francisco Focus* 1990

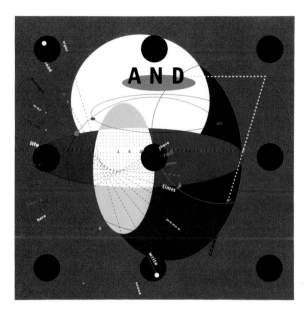

Brochure
AND Communications

Art Director/Designer
REVERB Lisa Nugent

© *AND Communications* 1991

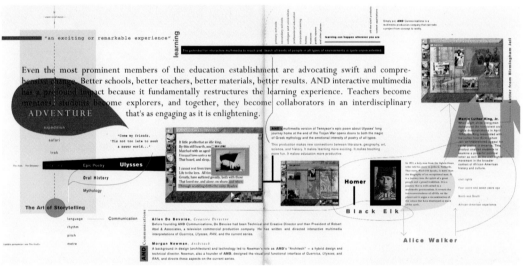

Magazine Spread
The Boston Globe
Supplement

Art Director/Designer
Rena Sokolow

Photographer
Sharon Roberts

© *The Boston Globe
Newspaper Co.* 1993

A secure environment for your records!

24 Hrs.

The key to record storage!

Off-site

Record Management

Brochure
Off-Site Record Management
Art Director/Designer/Illustrator
Earl Gee
© *Earl Gee* 1990

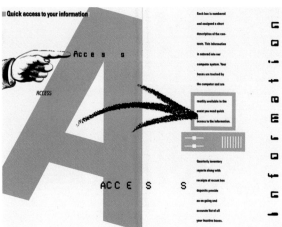

Quick access to your information

Booklets
Public Eye

Designer
David Cowles

Illustrators
David Cowles
Chris Fisher
Maria Friske
A. Skwish

© *David Cowles* 1992

Richard Hess, Larger than Life. Presented by Mark Hess. With video commentary from Sam Antupit, David Brown, Lou Dorfsman, Milton Glaser and Miho. November 18 1992, 7-9 pm. The Katie Murphy Amphitheatre, Fashion Institute of Technology, 227 West 27th Street, at 7th Avenue, New York, New York. Members $5, Non members $5, $1 left on the other side of the door. **M**any of his peers believed that he came from the West- it is part of his myth. But in fact he was born, in 1934, in Royal Oak, Michigan. He inherited from his brawling, square-jawed,

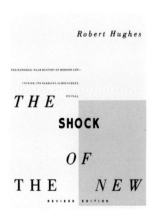

Robert Hughes

THE HUNDRED-YEAR HISTORY OF MODERN ART—

ITS RISE, ITS DAZZLING ACHIEVEMENT,

THE

SHOCK

ITS FALL

OF

THE   NEW

REVISED EDITION

Poster
Richard Hess

Designer
Robert Appleton

Photographers
Tom Hollyman *color*
Dmitri Kasterine *b/w*

© *AIGA/NY* 1992

Book Cover
The Shock of the New

Designer
Chip Kidd

© *Chip Kidd* 1990

19

the means of

Expression

The
Common
denominator

PostScript software is more than the industry standard for computer printers. It is the foundation of Adobe technology, growing more rapidly today than ever before. Hundreds of output devices and thousands of programs incorporate PostScript language technology, which now supports a new generation of performance and features with PostScript Level 2, including high-quality fax transmission. No matter what the digital communications need, the best answer includes PostScript software from Adobe.

that continues TO

multiply

[POSTSCRIPT IS THE LINGUA FRANCA OF THE COMPUTER WORLD]

A new Type

technology

Annual Report
Adobe Systems Incorporated

Creative Directors
Aubrey Balkind
Kent Hunter

Designer
Kin Yuen

Illustrator
Henrik Drescher *above right*

© *Adobe Systems Incorporated* 1993

Book Jacket
Sylvia Plachy's Unguided Tour

Designer
Yolanda Cuomo

Photographer
Sylvia Plachy

© *Aperture Foundation* 1990

Magazine Spread
Rolling Stone

Art Director
Fred Woodward

Designer
Debra Bishop

Letterer
Anita Karl

Photographer
Andrew Eccles

© *Wenner Media, Inc.* 1991

Magazine Spread
Rolling Stone

Art Director
Fred Woodward

Designers
Fred Woodward
Gail Anderson

Illustrator
Al Hirschfeld

© *Wenner Media, Inc.* 1993

Book Jacket
My Hard Bargain

Designer/Photographer
Chip Kidd

© *Chip Kidd* 1989

Book Jacket
Out of Work

Designer
Archie Ferguson

Photographer
Anne Turyn

© *Alfred A. Knopf* 1993

Poster
Big P Little O, Little O Big P

Art Director
Paula Scher

Designers
Ron Louie
Paula Scher

© *Pentagram* 1992

22

advance reading sample

21

twenty-one

collected stories

Ward Just

Book Cover
Ward Just: 21 Collected Stories

Art Director/Designer
Paula Scher

© *Pentagram* 1990

the next sounds you hear >

VOLUME 1

Promotional CD/Package
The Next Sounds You Hear

Art Director/Designer
Frank Gargiulo

Photographer
Diana Klein

© *Atlantic Recording Corp.* 1993

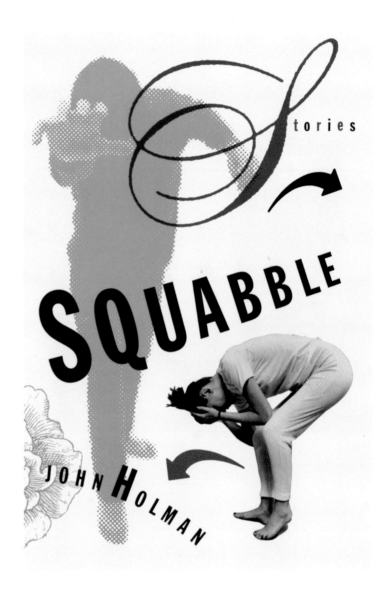

Book Cover
Hats

Designer
Helene Silverman

Photographer
John Dugdale

© *Clarkson Potter* 1991

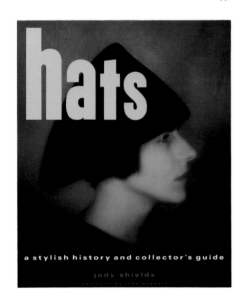

Book Jacket
Squabble

Art Director
Sara Eiseman

Designer
Carin Goldberg

Photographer
Benno Friedman

© *Houghton Mifflin* 1990

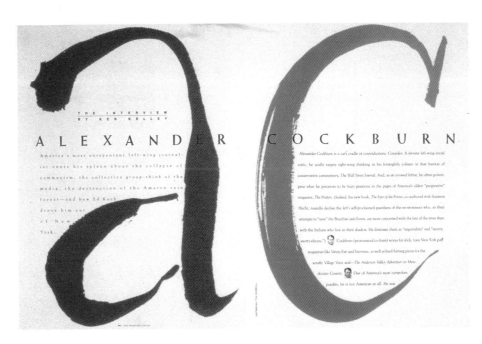

Poster
The Big A

Art Director/Designer
Paula Scher

© *Pentagram* 1991

Magazine Spread
San Francisco Focus

Art Director/Designer
Matthew Drace

Letterer
Tim Carroll

© *San Francisco Focus* 1990

Chapter 2

Changes in design begin at the edges and cut their way, often on a jagged course, toward the center. In typography, like any other visible visual art, change is accepted timidly at first, then as it gathers momentum the adherents grow in number. The more the new is seen, the less the shock is felt, and with enough followers the edge eventually dulls. History shows that challenges to the typographic canon have been wed to changes in basic form. Given that type is a mediator of language the degree to which change takes place is limited. In recent years as the notion of typographic neutrality has been seriously debated, and the computer has made typographic personality ever more possible, those on the cutting edge have aggressively played with expressionistic approaches. While much of what has been produced is too personal for widespread use, the lessons learned from these experiments have become a foundation for further exploration. The pioneers of expressionistic form have proven that rules of type are not only mutable but often irrelevant. They have also proposed that in addition to being a servant of meaning, typography can invoke its own meaning. Some cutting edge typography is built on the necessary foundation that discovery is a natural order, some is merely the regurgitation of what has been adopted as style. Perhaps only time will tell what work will have legs and what will be artifice. The cutting edge of the past five years has been accused of crimes against qualitative standards, but in the end—whether effective or not the lessons learned from the cutting edge are endemic to the viability of contemporary typography.

CUT-TING-TING

EDGE

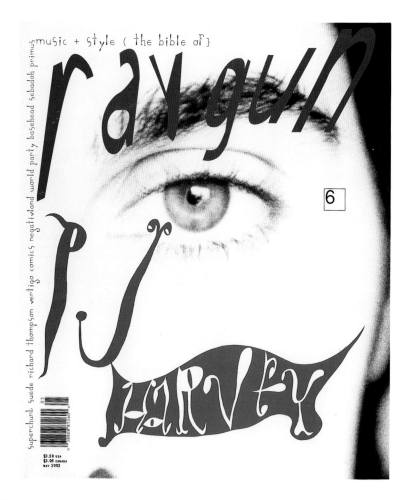

ray gun

superchunk suede richard thompson vertigo comics negativland world party basehead sebadoh primus

6

PJ Harvey

$3.50 USA
$3.95 CANADA
MAY 1993
05

Magazine Cover/Spread
Ray Gun

Designer
David Carson

Hand Letterer
Calef Brown *right*

Photographers
Colin Bell *right*
Skid *below*

© *David Carson Design* 1993

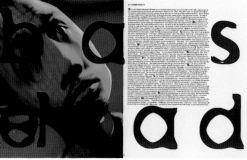

Magazine Spread
Beach Culture

Designer
David Carson

© *David Carson Design* 1991

28

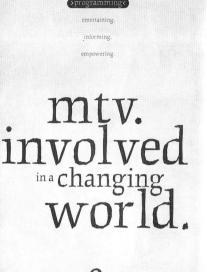

‹programming›

entertaining.

informing.

empowering.

mtv.
involved
in a changing
world.

Media Kit
MTV

Creative Directors
Aubrey Balkind
Kent Hunter

Designers
Andreas Combuchen
Johan Vipper

© *MTV Networks* 1992

‹ SPECIALS ›

only the
biggest **stars.**
only the biggest
events.
only on
MTV.

› Led by the highly rated MTV Video Music Awards, MTV Specials have broken through
to become some of the biggest events on the small screen.

‹research›

facts.
figures.
truth.

mtv. the
passion
is
mutual.

Studio Gift
Smoke Bomb in Bag

Designers
SMOKEBOMB STUDIO
Nancy Mazzei, Brian Kelly

© *Smokebomb Studio* 1993

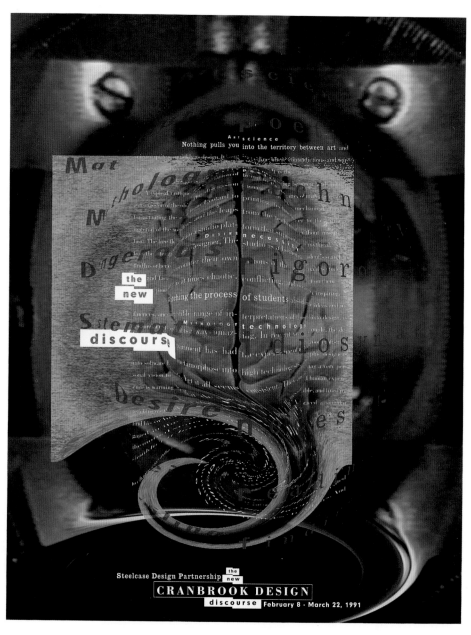

Poster
Incite Insight

Designer
Margo Chase

Photographer
Merlyn Rosenberg

© *Margo Chase* 1992

Poster
Cranbrook Design

Designer
P. Scott Makela

© *P. Scott Makela* 1989-90

Magazine Spread
Beach Culture

Designer
David Carson

Photographer
Art Brewer

© *David Carson Design* 1991

Record/Cover
Second Hand Rhythm Tool

Designers
SMOKEBOMB STUDIO
Nancy Mazzei, Brian Kelly

© *Smokebomb Records* 1993

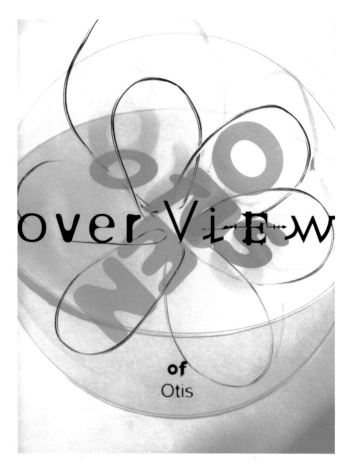

Brochure/Poster
Overview of Otis

Designer
REVERB Lisa Nugent

Photographers
Lisa Nugent
Steve Callis

© *Otis College* 1992

Magazine Cover
Design Quarterly

Designer
P. Scott Makela

Design Assistant
Alex Tylevich

© *P. Scott Makela* 1993

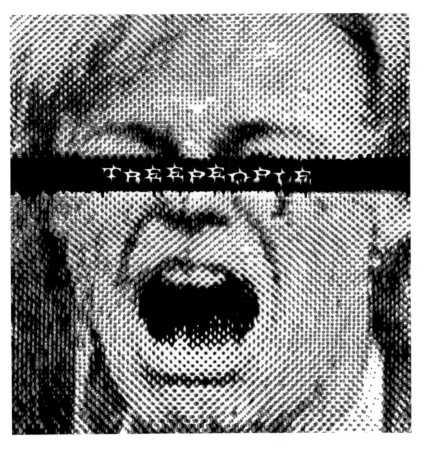

Book Cover
Treepeople

Designer
Art Chantry

© *Art Chantry* 1992

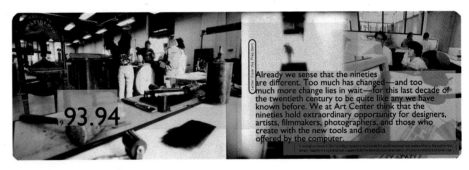

Catalog
Art Center College of Design

Creative Director
Stuart I. Frolick

Designer
Rebeca Mendez

Associate Designers
Darren Namaye
Darin Beaman

Photographer
Steven A. Heller

© *Art Center College of Design* 1992

Sales of
$2.8 billion,
earnings
per share of
$1.56,
and net income
of $88 million
represent
record
operating
performance.

John M. Kucharski
Chairman of the Board and Chief Executive Officer

56	Management's Responsibility for the Financial Statements
57	Segment Sales and Income
58	Management's Discussion and Analysis
61	Selected Financial Information
62	Consolidated Balance Sheet
63	Consolidated Statement of Income
64	Consolidated Statement of Stockholders' Equity
65	Consolidated Statement of Cash Flows
66	Notes to Consolidated Financial Statements
66	1. Summary of Significant Accounting Policies
67	2. Acquisitions
67	3. Accounts Receivable
67	4. Inventories
68	5. Property, Plant and Equipment, at Cost
68	6. Investments
68	7. Intangible and Other Assets
69	8. Debt
69	9. Accrued Expenses
70	10. Stockholders' Equity
71	11. Research and Development
71	12. Employee Benefit Plans
73	13. Leases
73	14. Other Income (Expense), Net
74	15. Income Taxes
75	16. Earnings Per Share
75	17. Industry Segment and Geographic Area Information
77	18. Summarized Quarterly Results of Operations (Unaudited)
77	19. Contingencies
78	Report of Independent Public Accountants

-55-

Annual Report
EG&G

Art Director
FRANKFURT BALKIND PARTNERS
Kent Hunter

Creative Directors
FRANKFURT BALKIND PARTNERS
Aubrey Balkind, Kent Hunter

Designers
FRANKFURT BALKIND PARTNERS
Andreas Combuchen, Hans Neubert

© *EG&G* 1993

34

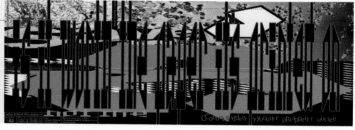

Brochure
Gilbert Paper

Designer
THIRST

© *THIRST* 1993

music+style
(the bible of)
PREMIERE ISSUE

henry rollins
sonic youth
house of love
inspiral carpets
john wesley
harding
the lemonheads
luna
opus 111
the prodigy
mary's danish
mission uk
too much joy
david j
matt mahurin

rAY Gun

Magazine Cover
Ray Gun

Art Director/Designer
David Carson

Illustrator
Larry Carroll

© *David Carson Design* 1993

Magazine Cover
Ray Gun

Art Director/Designer
David Carson

Photographer
Matt Mahurin

© *David Carson Design* 1993

FREEDOM IS IT! YOU'RE SO SCARED, YOU WANT TO LOCK UP EVERYBODY.
ARE THEY MAD DOGS? ARE THEY OUT TO KILL? MAYBE YES.
IS LAW, IS ORDER THE SOLUTION? DEFINITELY NO. WHAT CAUSED THIS SITUATION?
LACK OF FREEDOM. WHAT HAPPENS NOW? LET PEOPLE FULFILL THEIR NEEDS.
IS FREEDOM CONSTRUCTIVE OR IS IT DESTRUCTIVE? THE ANSWER IS OBVIOUS.
FREE PEOPLE ARE GOOD, PRODUCTIVE PEOPLE. IS LIBERATION DANGEROUS?
ONLY WHEN OVERDUE. PEOPLE AREN'T BORN RABID OR BERSERK.
WHEN YOU PUNISH AND SHAME YOU CAUSE WHAT YOU DREAD. WHAT TO DO?
LET IT EXPLODE. RUN WITH IT. DON'T CONTROL OR MANIPULATE. MAKE AMENDS.

Poster
Smokebomb Promo #1

Designers
SMOKEBOMB STUDIO
Nancy Mazzei, Brian Kelly

© *Smokebomb Studio* 1992

music, bible, style etc

Ray Gun

ig 8 gy

august 1993
usa $3.50
canada $3.95

Book Spread
Rethinking Design: Doing Nothing

Designer
P. Scott Makela

© *P. Scott Makela* 1992-93

End Papers
Facing New York

Designers
Yolanda Cuomo
Naomi Winegrad

© *Bruce Gilden and*
Cornerhouse Publications 1992

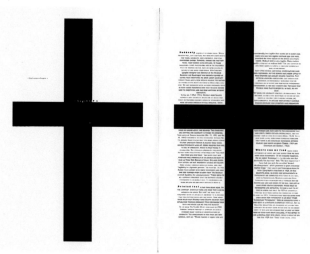

Magazine Spread
Emigre

Art Director/Designer
Rudy Vanderlans

© *Emigre* 1992

And so a graphic designer, although one may be antisocial, cannot not be social, cannot be isolationist.

To work as a designer means taking part in the discussion as an individual.

The discussion may be intimate, it may be very public, but most of all, it is an individual speaking with others.

It follows then that to join the discussion or to be conversational, an individual must have a voice. In order to converse effectively—or rather to effectively contribute to a conversation as an individual—the attitude of the voice or her or his' identity needs to be readily apparent.

Designers should take a stand, express a point of view; their work should make transparent politics, bias, passions, emotions.

Since a graphic designer "converses" through a printed work, it is especially easy now, with the everyday use of computers in design, to unveil the designer's personal thinking process—by leaving traces and ends of production in the final result—simply leaving evidence within the finished product of the physical process (an ironically hand-crafted quality). it is possible for designers to actually represent a discourse.

The antithesis of individual representation within graphic design is the corporate logo. In "The Rise and Fall of the Corporate Identity", Ken Garland argues that the corporate logo cannot represent any one thing or person. In fact, Garland continues, that the most successful and obscene use of the logo was by the Nazi party.

"Corporate identity," Garland claims, "is infused with over-weaning, elitist notions of power and the imposition of power by the visionary few."

Yet in order to represent everything, corporate identities become too diffuse, too bland, too all-encompassing.

In a lecture delivered at Brunswick in May 1910, he stated: "It is particularly important for Germany, which has now achieved political power, also to win power in artistic areas...In this way, German art and technology will work towards one goal: towards the power of the German nation, which reveals itself in a rich material life ennobled by intellectually refined design."

FRIGHTENINGLY WELL DESIGNED So here's our paragon: even at its inception, corporate identity is infused with over-weaning, elitist notions of power and the imposition of order by the visionary few. It is no coincidence, I feel, that within a quarter of a century of this statement, the most effective and arguably the best designed corporate identity of the twentieth century was the one that represented the most effective, and arguably the best organized, socio-political system of the twentieth century; nor that it arose in Germany and that it was imbued with Nietzschean concepts of the UBERMENSCH.

It was also the most obscene of all totalitarian regimes. This tempts the question: is it only the monolithic, all-powerful organizations like AEG or the Nazi Party which can make really effective use of corporate identity? Certainly, the near-monopoly of AEG gave the company an assurance that was immensely helpful to Behrens in his design program. And the total control exercised by the Nazi regime over its workforce and the availability of resources was equally important to Albert Speer in his impressive devices of corporate identity at great gatherings like the Nuremberg Rallies and in bombastic city planning exercises like the 1939 North-South Axis in Berlin (to which, incidentally Behrens contributed his last architectural work: an office building for AEG).

The proposition is also born out by a number of postwar examples of which the corporate identity program for IBM by Eliot Noyes, as design director, and Paul Rand as design consultant, was—and still is—a model. IBM offers a prime illustration of the contention that, however well designed, a ubiquitous and successful corporate identity is ultimately a calamity just BECAUSE it is ubiquitous. That's the bitter lesson we've only just begun to learn.

" is infused with over-weaning, elitist notions of power and the imposition of power by the visionary few. "

When we shower the design periodicals and quality newspapers with angry complaints about the blowsy bugler of BT, we are still missing the point. True, the BT style is an even more footling bit of nonsense than the Prudential popinjay, also from the same design office. But any corporate identity that puts itself about as ostentatiously as these two is offensive, whatever it looks like.

NO MORE CASH FOR CANDYFLOSS
So what's to be done? Well, to some extent the problem has solved itself. I cannot believe that any large company will be prepared to fling its money about on candyfloss graphics from now on. Assuming, therefore, that it can be justifiably channelled in our ...er portion of it can... throw in our lot with ...direction? For starters, we... those local authorities, civic amenity groups, town planners and others concerned with the depredations of multinational companies, hypermarkets and recently "liberated" public utilities who have been allowed to blazon their insistent company image over our towns and countryside with minimum control from central government. With them, we can promote the idea of the spirit of the place. Not a new idea, of course; it's probably as old as the first human society. It is a vital part of the training and development of the architect; why not of graphic designers now that they may have as much or more influence on the appearance of some environments?

Then we could attempt to persuade the multinationals and other biggies that swanking around the globe about their bigness is increasingly counter-productive. I wouldn't be surprised if it hasn't occurred to them already: they're probably ahead of us. Imagine the embarrassment when we turn up at the board room with our next Corp ID proposals and various facets of a given corporation and the hard men frown at it and say, "Bit monolithic, isn't it? Does it have to be quite so ostentatious?" And can we divest ourselves of some of the gruesome hangers-on in our business: the rejects from ad agencies and sales departments who've conned us into thinking that they, rather than we, have their fingers on the pulse of business and industry.

Finally, I offer you Garland's Law of Corporate Identity: that the degree of memorability and distinction applicable to any organization should be in inverse ratio to the size of its annual profits or the size of its chief executive's salary, whichever is the greater.

There's no reason for corporations to employ such monolithic identities. Perhaps corporate identities could be broken down into a system of logos to closer represent different individuals of a given corporation.

Although of "visual babel" illiteracy are being hurled from all sides, at the same time there for designers... the demise of... corporate identity by...

The successful graphic designer is, in short, inspired to create—and cultivating individual identities (and peculiarities, "character," personal style) make every effort to see that his creation reaches out to the —that is, to be truly viewer with meaning." conversational in their work.

Chapter 3

Before phototypography came of age in the late 1960s there was little attempt at distorting typefaces. Yet the idea of stretching, pulling, and otherwise contorting a headline or text block was not unheard of. Designers working in hot metal interested in exploring this avenue of expression attempted cumbersome processes to do their dirty work. With the widespread introduction of phototypesetting machines in the sixties—notably the Phototypositor—letters could be smashed, overlapped, and otherwise toyed with at will. The availability of anamorphic lenses contributed to, indeed encouraged such play instincts. But what was the reason for distortion? Was it merely vandalism or was there a viable goal? Perhaps both. For some designers distortion was youthful mischief, not unlike scrawling graffiti on a billboard. For others it was rebellion against typographic tradition. With the advent of digital technology distortion became even easier, if not more in demand. While this too suggests a certain amount of mischievousness among young designers, cut with a bit of rebellion, distortion today is a function, indeed a code, of the times. Distortion comes naturally on television and video screens. Where once legibility depended on perceiving the sharp edges of letterforms surrounded by ample negative space, one can now discern word-images in motion. Like military spotters, who are trained to identify planes, ships or cars from their fast-moving silhouettes, readers today are able to derive meaning from kinetic letterforms. People are used to being bombarded with moving words, and therefore can read in spite of the distortion. The deliberate contortion of today's letterforms builds upon this new, shall we say evolutionary, skill. But it is also a means of exploring new realms of perception. Distortion provides new textures against which designers can at once test legibility and create new visual paradigms. Although not a suitable method for all communications, distorted faces can enliven print by extending its boundaries.

DISTORTED FACES

Logo
Bryce Goggin Recording

Designers
SMOKEBOMB STUDIO
Nancy Mazzei, Brian Kelly

© *Smokebomb Studio* 1992

On-Air Logo
MTV Spring Break

Designers
SMOKEBOMB STUDIO
Nancy Mazzei, Brian Kelly

© *Smokebomb Studio* 1992

CD Package
Trance Fusion

Designers/Illustrators
SMOKEBOMB STUDIO
Nancy Mazzei, Brian Kelly

© *Sonic Records* 1993

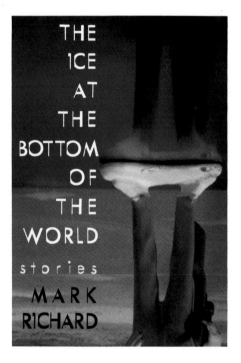

Record Cover Logo
Whiskey for the Holy Ghost

Designer
Art Chantry

© *Art Chantry* 1993

Book Jacket
The Ice at the Bottom of
the World

Designer
Chip Kidd

Photographer
Drew Pleak

© *Chip Kidd* 1989

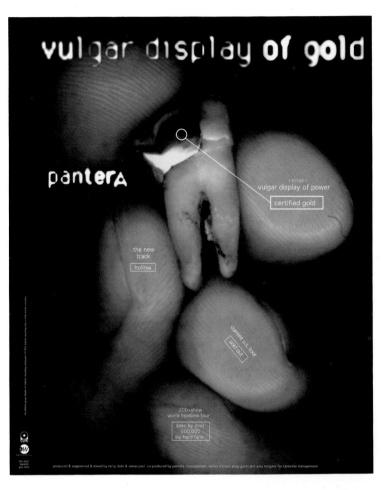

Advertisement
Pantera Gold

Designer/Photographer
Charlie Becker

© *Atlantic Recording Corp.* 1993

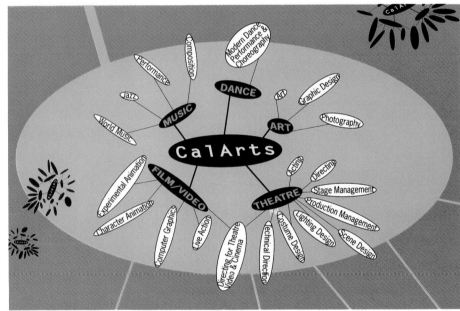

CD Package
Time for a Change

Designer
Steve Boyd

© *Bar / None Records, Inc.* 1989

Postcard
Cal Arts

Designer
Somi Kim

© *California Institute of the Arts* 1990

Book Jacket
William Burroughs: A Biography
Designer
Louise Fili
© *Louise Fili* 1993

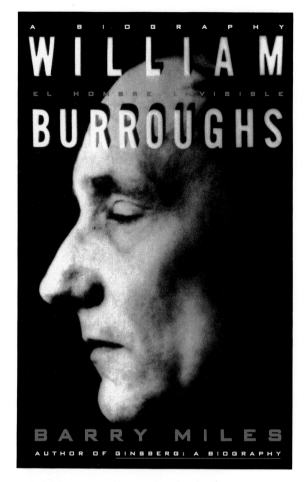

Book Jacket
Bone

Art Director
Victor Weaver

Designer
Carin Goldberg

© *Hyperion Books* 1993

CD/Package
700 Miles

Art Directors
Ria Lewerke
Jackie Murphy

Designer
Sean Smith

Photographer
Josef Komdelka

© *BMG Music* 1993

Poster
Bomb the Pentagon

Designer/Illustrator/Letterer
BLACKDOG Mark Fox

© *Mark Fox/BlackDog* 1991

Logo
Detroit Pistons

Art Director
NBA Tom O'Grady

Designer/Letterer
BLACKDOG Mark Fox

© *Mark Fox/BlackDog* 1992

Magazine Spread
Emigre

Art Director/Designer
Rudy Vanderlans

Photographer
THIRST Rick Valicenti

© *Emigre* 1989

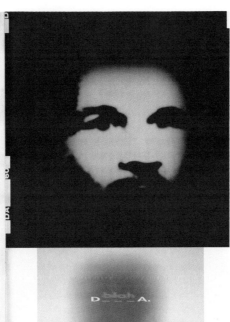

Johnny B: *Hey, what's going on?* Emigre: I just want to hear your reaction to this page we received from Thirst. Rick Valicenti just....Johnny: *Who?* Emigre: Eh...Rick Valicenti, he designed this page and he used Mike Ditka as a symbol for Chicago. Johnny: *Oh, yeah I saw that.* Emigre: Now, Ditka is not exactly the most popular guy around at this point. Three losses in a row! How do you feel about Ditka as a symbol for Chicago? Johnny: *It's a bit weird especially when I see Ditka talk on Monday Night Football, sorta going Blah, Blah, Blah... But personally I think it's a great tribute to the guy. Because eh...sports is my life, you know: graphic design, I like it, I know a bit about it, but sports is my life, and I love the coach. You know, he's a real strong personality. Unfortunately things aren't going so well at present. So he loses three games. So what? He'll be back. He's pissed right now, because you know, he's never lost three games in a row. But the guy never gives up, never says no, he never quits. Chicago likes that and coach Ditka stands for what this city is all about. We're a real blue collar town. It's a tough place. Not like San Francisco, those wimps. They have an earthquake and they cancel the World Series, the fucking WORLD SERIES! Come on! Sports is my life, I couldn't deal with that.* Emigre: So you think Ditka's sorry he traded McMahon right now? Johnny: *Well, I know Mike Ditka, II mean not personally, of course, we wouldn't get along. But eh...maybe in the back of his mind he might regret it a little bit. I don't know. Ditka's unpredictable. That's what we like about the guy. And anyhow, in San Diego they're gonna bench McMahon this Sunday. So what's there to be sorry about?!* Emigre: What do you think Valicenti means with that type on the bottom? Johnny: *Yeah, I'm a little bit pissed off about that, cause he's not clear about it. Is he making fun of the coach there with those letters at the bottom, 'DA, blah?' I don't know...* Emigre: Well, what do you think he means by that? Johnny: *How the hell would I know?!* Well maybe it's about how the coach is CHICAGO / Rick Valicenti [Thirst] always on television going like blah, blah, blah. He's always mouth'n off a lot. But eh...he's a motivator, he brings out the best in people. Sometimes he's aggressive, sometimes he's happy, sometimes he's selling cars, sometimes Tristan or house mortgages. Anything! But I think Valicenti's interpretation is eh... you know, what is the coach really saying? And it looks like you got a four letter word there or something. Emigre: So you like the idea of replacing the Sears Tower with Ditka's face? Johnny: *Yeah, to hell with the Sears Tower. Ditka has a very strong presence in town. You see him everywhere, in the papers, on the news, all the time, the guy's everywhere.* Emigre: What do you think of that shot Valicenti used? Taken off a television screen, that's not the most flattering picture is it? At least he could have used some sort of promotional 8 by 10 glossy? Johnny: *Nah. Well, you know, on the one hand I say great, Ditka's face as a symbol. Chicago's big brother, in the city of big shoulders; that's great. But he's not making fun of the guy, or is he? But I guess coach Ditka does the same thing. That's the best part of it. He's talking to the press everyday, the cameras are on him all the time, he'll stick a piece of gum on the camera, he'll do this or that, he's always poking fun, and he's always on TV.* Emigre: So you consider this to be an appropriate design? Johnny: *What? You're asking for my approval? Is that it?* Emigre: Well, is it thumbs up for this one? Johnny: *Yeah, sure, come on, the coach gets a full page in some graphic design magazine, I think that's great! Although I don't know what the hell's going on in there. What the hell's that all about? You got strange photos and textures here and there. I don't know what route you guys travel on your way to work, and shit, that rag costs quite a fortune, I mean jeezus!* Emigre: Well the moment we can produce it for fifty cents a copy we'll sell them for two bucks a piece. Johnny: *Nah, don't worry, I like that entrepreneurial attitude, take whatever you can get. Anyway, I gotta check out. Talk to you later, and eh... don't forget about the friggin' World Series on Friday night, OK? LaDeDa.*

Chapter 4

Before movable type the scribe was the principal letterer. Before phototypography the hand letterer, the descendant of the Medieval scribe, was the primary creator of informal letterforms. Hand lettering is an ancient and highly respected ability. In the 1920s and '30s before photostats were prevalent (or cost-efficient) the most skilled typographers rendered even the most standardized display typefaces by hand in arrangements that suited their purposes. For the late Moderns mixing formal faces with suggestive hand lettering was a way of adding humor to their work. In the wake of the digital explosion hand lettering has atrophied somewhat, but talented letterers are still in demand to create, indeed invent, forms that are either too difficult for the computer to accomplish or simply where the need is for hand-over mechanical work. Although achieving the perfect hand-lettered piece is not easy—once a style or manner is determined meticulous planning is necessary to get the right result—some examples look as though they instantaneously materialized. Yet for hand lettering to be virtuous today, it must look like it was done by hand—a somewhat archaic idea in the digital age. This means that despite the excruciating pain to produce the perfect letterforms, some imperfection must be noticeable to the tutored, and even untutored eye. On the other side of the coin, hand lettering is also a symbol of defiance against the encroachment of technology. In an era when perfect typefaces can be "drawn" on the screen, the unfaltering human hand suggests a mastery of the form. Yet there is a third manifestation for hand lettering in concert with (and reproduced by) computer-aided technology. In the anything-goes design environment the combination of formal and informal letterforms is a means of injecting texture into what otherwise might be one-dimensional work. The hand-lettered form allows the designer to break from the rigid strictures of "pure typography."

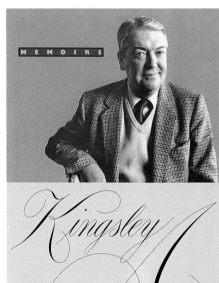

CD Package
Mr. Wendal

Designer
Randall Martin

Photographer
Keith Ward

© Chrysalis Records,
a division of EMI
Records Group, NA 1992

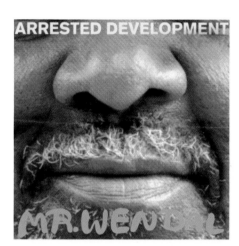

CD Package
Natural

Designers
Marc Cozza
Randall Martin

Photographer
Sheila Turner

© Chrysalis Records,
a division of EMI
Records Group, NA 1993

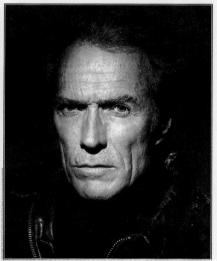

Magazine Spread
Rolling Stone

Art Director/Designer
Fred Woodward

Letterer
Anita Karl

Photographer
Albert Watson

© Wenner Media, Inc. 1992

Magazine Cover
New York

Art Director
Syndi Becker

Design Direcor
Robert Best

Designer/Letterer
Anthony Bloch

© Anthony Bloch 1992

Magazine Spread
Rolling Stone

Art Director
Fred Woodward

Designer/Letterer
Gail Anderson

Photographer
David Katzenstein

© *Wenner Media, Inc.* 1990

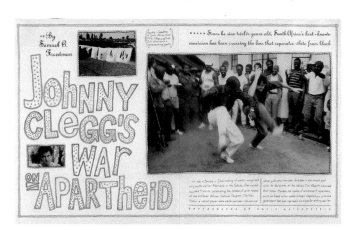

48

Magazine Page
Rolling Stone

Art Director/Designer
Fred Woodward

Photographer
Bruce Weber

© *Wenner Media, Inc.* 1990

Sales Kit
Plan It for the Planet

Art Director
Julie Wilson

Designer
Michelle Willems

© *Nickelodeon* 1993

Logo
Private Clubs

Designer/Letterer
Bernard Maisner

© Bernard Maisner 1990

49

Logo
New York Zoological Society

Designer/Letterer
Bernard Maisner

© Bernard Maisner 1991

Lettering for Book Cover
The Many Lives of Elton John

Designer/Illustrator
Bernard Maisner

Publisher
Carol Publishing Group

© Bernard Maisner 1992

Logo
Taverna Christina

Designer
Scott Ray

© *Peterson & Company* 1986

Record Logo
The Leon Thomas Blues Band

Designer/Letterer
Bernard Maisner

Record Company
CBS Records

© *Bernard Maisner* 1990

Logo
Mark Ryden Illustration

Designer
Mark Ryden

© *Mark Ryden* 1992

Poster
Rosarito-Ensenada Bicycle Ride

Designer/Illustrator
Gerald Bustamante

© Gerald Bustamante 1992

Magazine Cover
Rolling Stone

Art Director/Designer
Fred Woodward

Letterer
Laurie Rosenwald

Photographer
Mark Seliger

© Wenner Media, Inc. 1991

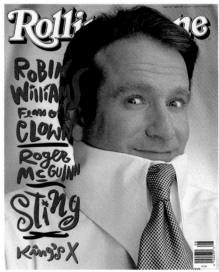

51

Poster
U.S.C.

Art Director/Designer
Laurie Rosenwald

Publisher
University of Southern California

© Rosenwald/U.S.C. 1992

Poster
Cosmic Thing

Art Director/Designer
Pat Gorman

Letterer
Frank Olinsky

Photographer
Virginia Liberatore

© *Manhattan Design/*

Virginia Liberatore 1989

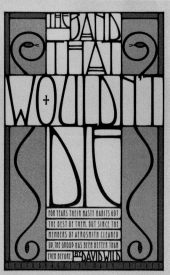

Magazine Spread
Rolling Stone

Art Director
Fred Woodward

Designer
Debra Bishop

Letterer
Anita Karl

Photographer
Mark Seliger

© *Wenner Media, Inc.* 1990

Logo
Nordstrom Sales Mark

Designer
Art Chantry

© *Art Chantry* 1987

Poster
Moonshake

Art Director
Marko

Designers
SMOKEBOMB STUDIO
Nancy Mazzei, Brian Kelly

© *Matador Records* 1993

Book Jacket
The Lover

Art Director/Designer
Louise Fili

Hand Letterer
Craig de Camps

© *Louise Fili* 1984

53

Magazine Cover
San Francisco Focus

Art Director/Designer
Matthew Drace

Illustrator/Letterer
Tim Carroll

© *San Francisco Focus* 1990

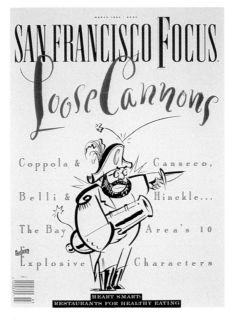

Chapter 5

Unlike hand lettering, which even when seemingly informal is based on formal constructs, handwriting is the most casual approach to lettering. Handwriting is to hand lettering or calligraphy what typewriter type is to typeface design. Most everyone has a handwriting style that develops in school from standardized approaches such as the Palmer Method. Like other personal characteristics, handwriting usually evolves consistent with the personality who is using it—and handwriting analysts are quick to point to certain

defining traits that speak volumes about the particular writer's character. As common as it is in everyday life, handwriting is not widely used in graphic design. Perhaps the informality of handwriting suggests a lack of authority. But periodically designers turn to handwriting as a plaything. They test its limits and stretch its boundaries; goose it, contort it, and caress it. In the 1950s, record designer Alex Steinweiss took his signature and developed it into a typeface that was humorously called "Steinweiss Scrawl." While most designers would not have the hubris to develop integrated alphabets from their own writing styles, occasionally a specific problem can be solved this way. In the 1970s numerous record albums and promotions, particularly those for solo recording artists, were adorned with handwriting as if to suggest a personal greeting from the soloist to the audience. Similarly, magazines used handwriting as headlines to indicate a more personal essay than the typical reportage. For some designers

handwriting was fast, cheap, and of course, expressive. Before the digital age many inexpensive alternative publications were replete with handwriting to offset other expenses. Today, however, with the plethora of cheap laser-printed type, using handwriting does not cut many corners. But in the atmosphere of experimentation and play, handwriting is still a way of personalizing graphic design.

Hand
writing

Album Cover
Slanted and Enchanted
Designer
PAVEMENT, INC. Stephen Malkmus
© *Matador Records* 1992

56

Book Jacket
A Quick Kiss of Redemption
and Other Stories
Art Director
Linda Koserin
Designer
Carin Goldberg
© *William Morrow* 1991

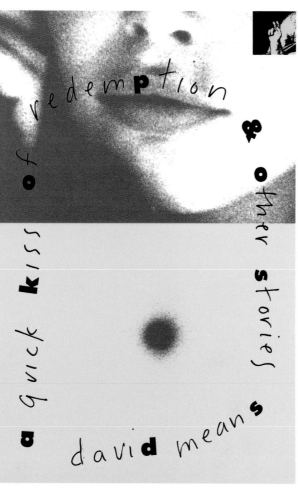

CD/Package
All Jets Are Gonna
Fall Today

Designers
CHOCOLATE USA
Lisa Wagner

© *Bar / None Records, Inc.* 1993

Record/Cover
Trigger Cut Plus Two
Designer
PAVEMENT, INC. Stephen Malkmus
© *Matador Records* 1992

Advertisement
Metal Multi
Designer/Illustrator
Charlie Becker

© *Atlantic Recording Corp.* 1993

Book Cover
Memoirs of an Anti-Semite

Art Director
Susan Mitchell

Designers
Marc Cohen
Susan Mitchell

Photographer
Angela Arnet

© *Random House, Inc.* 1991

Book Jacket
Kicking Tomorrow

Designer
Chip Kidd

© *Chip Kidd* 1989

58

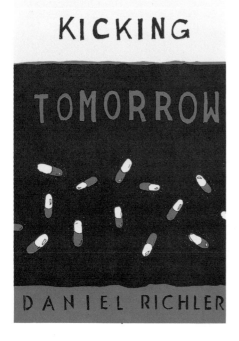

CD Package
The Full-Custom
Gospel Sounds of
the Rev. Horton Heat

Designer
Art Chantry

Photographer
James Bland

© *Art Chantry* 1993

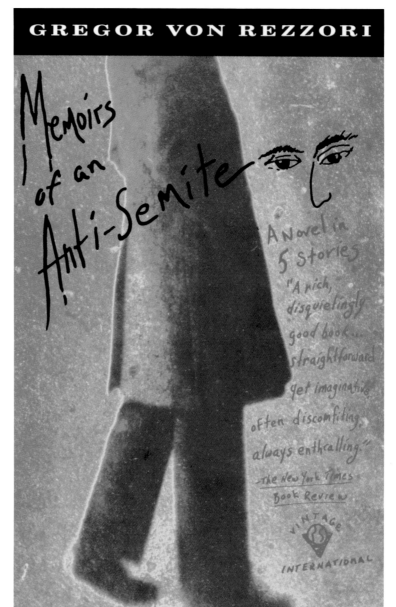

Book Jacket
Grey Is the Color of Hope
Designer
Chip Kidd
© *Chip Kidd* 1988

Book Jacket
Pencil Letter
Designer
Chip Kidd
© *Chip Kidd* 1989

Book Jacket
The Cover Artist

Art Directors
Carin Goldberg
Frank Metz

Illustrator/Letterer
Isabelle Derveaux

© *Simon & Schuster* 1991

Greeting Card
Big Stars

Designer
Laurie Rosenwald

© *Laurie Rosenwald and
Virgin Records America* 1991

See JANE demonstrate Thermography

See Jane spell
She CAN spell well
Can't you tell?

Ah, to win this spelling bee!
She WOULD if she COULD
But in all likelihood,
Her EARS are just no good!

OPEN YOUR EAR FLAPS!

What's THERMO-?

NO! the WORD was "GEOGRAPHY"

Promotional Brochure
See Jane Print

Art Director/Designer
ROBERT VALENTINE INC.

Illustrator
Jessie Hartland

©*Gilbert Paper* 1993

See DICK letterpress
with such finesse!
(it beats handpress)
But none the less,
it brought distress
to our princess.

Letterpress

The letters all fell
and made life hell
They soon began to melt
(a snafu that was smelt)
But it's FUN to letterpress
Hurrah for making a mess!

Comic Book Cover/Page
Snake Eyes
Designer
Jonathon Rosen

© *Jonathon Rosen* 1992

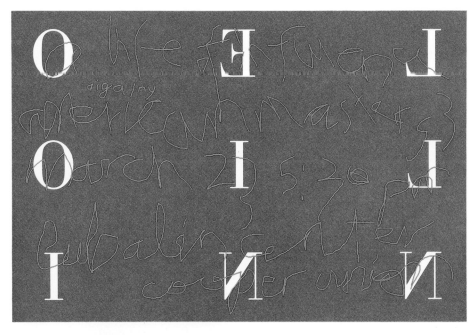

CD Package
Gravity Dance

Art Director
Pat Gorman

Illustrator
Henrik Drescher

© *Manhattan Design/Henrik Drescher* 1990

Postcard
Leo Lionni

Designer/Calligrapher
Robert Appleton

© *AIGA/NY* 1993

CD/Package
With My House

Art Director/Designer
Jean Cronin

Photographer
Lisa Peardon

© *Third Stone/Atlantic
Records* 1993

Chapter 6

In the 1960s smashed and overlapping letters indicated contemporaneity in graphic design. Phototypesetting made it possible for excruciatingly tight settings, which was an exceedingly difficult feat with hot metal. Traditionalists railed that this style was the downfall of typography, while progressives argued that it was merely a playful approach that hadn't been done because the technology was not previously available. In the end it had its proponents and adherents, was popular for a while, yet over time lost its novelty. The same has been said for the Jumbled Word school of typography. The layering, butting, and intersecting of headlines and body texts has been referred to as a pox on typography by the old school, but by the young it has long since transcended fashionable rebellion for status quo. Jumbled word or "rap typography," as one critic has pejoratively called it, is a rather appropriate manifestation in the current milieu. As smashed and overlapping letters symbolized the quick pace of the daily grind in the sixties, rap typography suggests the diverse public conversations in this ever expanding melting pot. While this does not mean that multiculturalism is the wellspring of jumbled words, it is a contributing factor. Actually, linguistic theory borrowed from academe is its primary source. The concept that language can be turned inside out, or deconstructed, to analyze meaning on various levels has given certain designers a motive for research and play. Jumbled words are at once a rejection of the Modern dictum for clean and simple communications, and have become emblematic of the reconfiguration of written language. In fact, in their pure form jumbled words are akin to footnotes, marginalia, or parentheticals, which are integrated into the text. And yet from these roots a mannerism has developed, sometimes good oftimes irrelevant, in which jumbled words have become nothing more or less than texture.

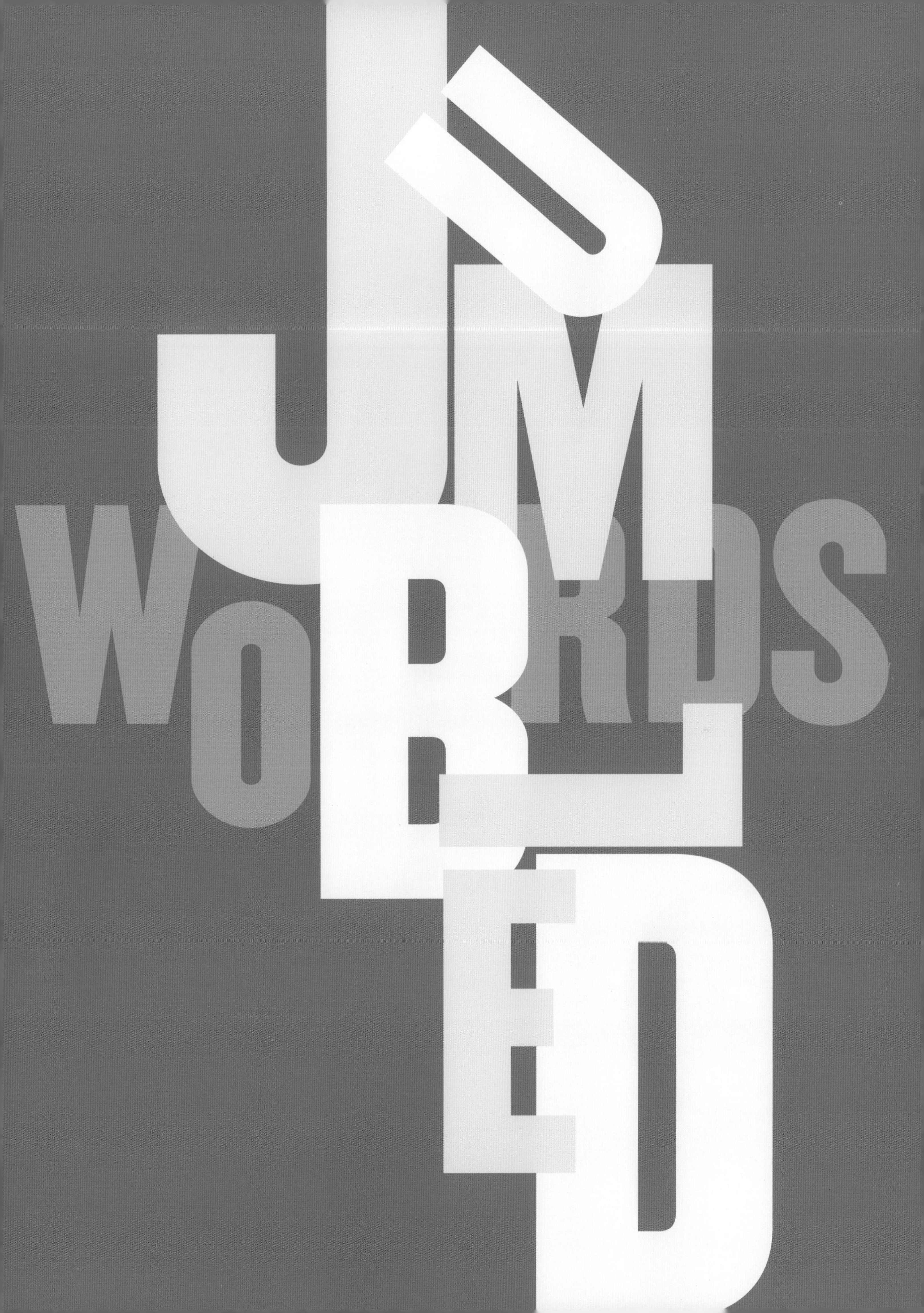
JUMBLED
WORDS

Book Spreads
Listen Up: The Lives of
Quincy Jones

Art Director
Helene Silverman

Design Director
FRANKFURT BALKIND PARTNERS
Kent Hunter

Designers
FRANKFURT BALKIND PARTNERS
Rike Sethiadi, Johan Vipper
Thomas Bricker

© *Courtney Sale Ross,
Quincy Jones* 1990

66

CD
Doo-Bop

Designer
Robin Lynch

Photographer
Annie Leibovitz

© *Warner Bros. Records* 1992

Logo
Red Hot Organization

Typeface/Logo Designers
Helene Silverman
Frank Gargiulo

© *Red Hot Organization* 1993

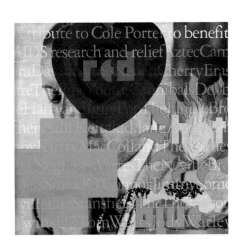

Album Cover
Red Hot and Blue

Art Director
Helene Silverman

Designer
Frank Gargiulo

© *Chrysalis* 1990

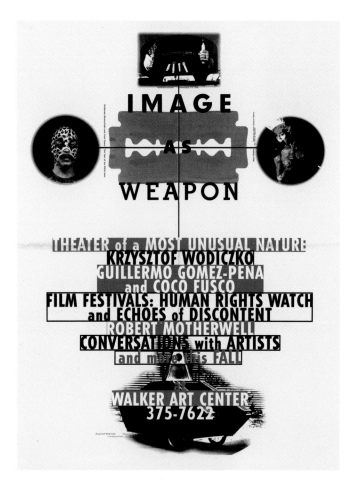

Poster/Brochure
Image as Weapon
Designer
P. Scott Makela

© *P. Scott Makela/WAC* 1992

Manual
The Knoll Group Identity Guidelines
Designer
CHERMAYEFF & GEISMAR, INC.
Cathy Schaefer

© *The Knoll Group* 1993

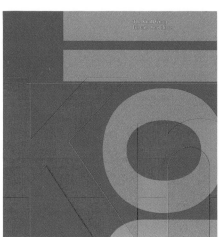

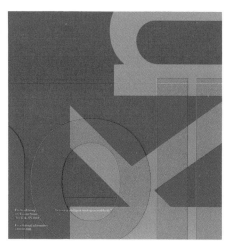

Magazine Spread
Rolling Stone

Art Director
Fred Woodward

Designers
Fred Woodward
Gail Anderson

Photographer
Mark Seliger

© *Wenner Media, Inc.* 1993

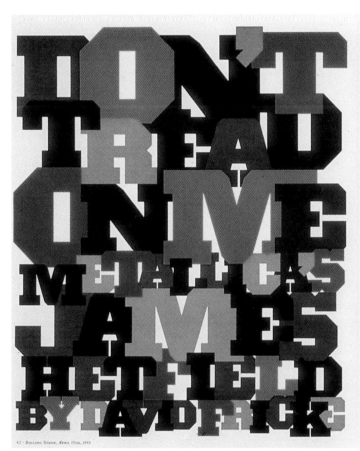

69

Book Jacket
The Rolling Stone
Illustrated History of Rock & Roll

Art Director/Designer
Fred Woodward

© *Random House, Inc.* 1992

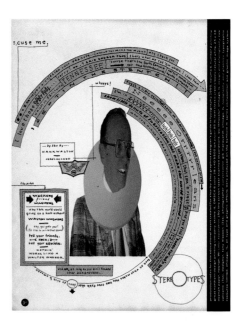

70

Magazine Pages
Step by Step

Designers
Rick Valicenti
Gib Marquardt

Photographer
Tony Klassen

© *THIRST* 1990

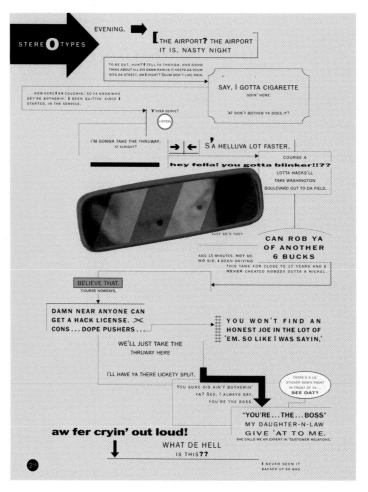

We believe passionately in the power of print

Brochure
Time Inc., Magazines

Creative Directors
FRANKFURT BALKIND PARTNERS
Danny Abelson, Kent Hunter

Designer
FRANKFURT BALKIND PARTNERS
Kin Yuen

© *Time Inc., Magazines* 1991

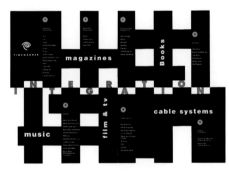

Logo
Montage

Designer
REVERB Somi Kim

© *Independent Feature
Project/West* 1990

Book Jacket
Trick or Treat

Art Director
Alexander Isley

Designer
Kay Schuckhart

Publisher
Clarkson Potter

© *Emily Gwathmey and
Suzanne Slesin* 1992

READING
& THE ARTS OF THE BOOK
— July 3, 1 9 9 2
onica, California

Lectures
The Getty Center for the History of Art and the Humanities
Panel Discussions
Demonstrations

From
The Getty Center for the History
of Art and the Humanities
401 Wilshire Boulevard Suite 400
Santa Monica California 90401-1455

To

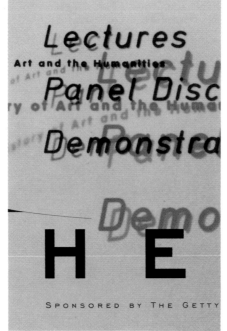

Lectures
the Getty Center for the History
Art and the Humanities
Panel Disc
Demonstra
Demo
OF THE
SPONSORED BY THE GETTY

Brochure
Reading and the Arts of the Book
Designer
REVERB Lisa Nugent
Photographer
Steve Callis

© *The Getty Center for Art and the*
Humanities 1992

Poster
Strategic Graphics Inc.

Designer
Robert Appleton

© *Strategic Graphics Inc.* 1992

73

Logo
Stark/Raving Theatre

Designer
Art Chantry

© *Art Chantry* 1992

Record Sleeve
Birdhouse in Your Soul

Designer
Helene Silverman

© *They Might Be Giants* 1990

CD Package
Kam, Neva Again

Art Director
Richard Bates

Designer
S. Sung Lee

Illustrator
Mac James

Photographer
Todd Gray

© *Atlantic Recording Corp.* 1993

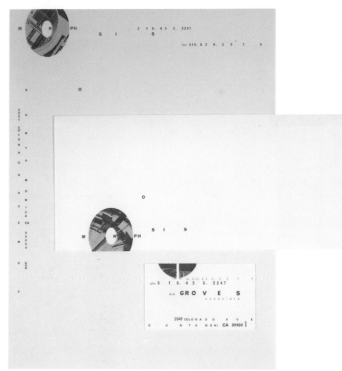

Album Cover
One Hell Soundwich

Art Director
Helene Silverman

Designer
Frank Gargiulo

Illustrators
Gary Panter
Jay Cotton

© *Blast First Records* 1990

Stationery
Morphosis

Designers
REVERB
Andrea Fella, Lorraine Wild
MORPHOSIS Thom Mayne

© *Morphosis* 1993

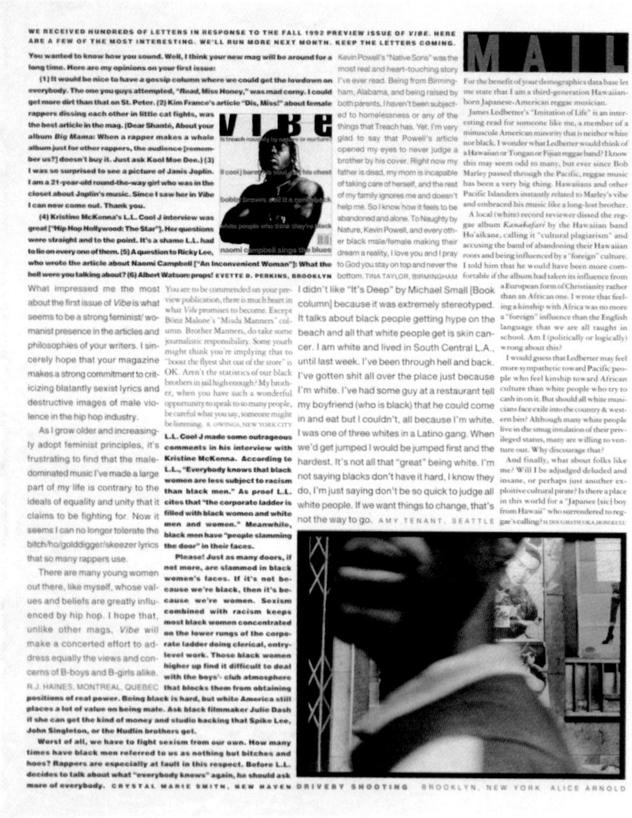

WE RECEIVED HUNDREDS OF LETTERS IN RESPONSE TO THE FALL 1992 PREVIEW ISSUE OF *VIBE*. HERE ARE A FEW OF THE MOST INTERESTING. WE'LL RUN MORE NEXT MONTH. KEEP THE LETTERS COMING.

MAIL

You wanted to know how you sound. Well, I think your new mag will be around for a long time. Here are my opinions on your first issue:

(1) It would be nice to have a gossip column where we could get the lowdown on everybody. The one you guys attempted, "*Read*, Miss Honey," was mad corny. I could get more dirt than that on St. Peter. (2) Kim France's article "Dis, Miss!" about female rappers dissing each other in little cat fights, was the best article in the mag. [Dear Shanté, About your album *Big Mama*: When a rapper makes a whole album just for other rappers, the audience [remember us?] doesn't buy it. Just ask Kool Moe Dee.] (3) I was so surprised to see a picture of Janis Joplin. I am a 21-year-old round-the-way girl who was in the closet about Joplin's music. Since I saw her in *Vibe* I can now come out. Thank you.

(4) Kristine McKenna's L.L. Cool J interview was great ["Hip Hop Hollywood: The Star"]. Her questions were straight and to the point. It's a shame L.L. had to lie on every one of them. (5) A question to Ricky Lee, who wrote the article about Naomi Campbell ["An Inconvenient Woman"]: What the hell were you talking about? (6) Albert Watson: props! EVETTE D. PERKINS, BROOKLYN

Kevin Powell's "Native Sons" was the most real and heart-touching story I've ever read. Being from Birmingham, Alabama, and being raised by both parents, I haven't been subjected to homelessness or any of the things that Treach has. Yet, I'm very glad to say that Powell's article opened my eyes to never judge a brother by his cover. Right now my father is dead, my mom is incapable of taking care of herself, and the rest of my family ignores me and doesn't help me. So I know how it feels to be abandoned and alone. To Naughty by Nature, Kevin Powell, and every other black male/female making their dream a reality, I love you and I pray to God you stay on top and never the bottom. TINA TAYLOR, BIRMINGHAM

For the benefit of your demographics data base let me state that I am a third-generation Hawaiian-born Japanese-American reggae musician.

James Ledbetter's "Imitation of Life" is an interesting read for someone like me, a member of a minuscule American minority that is neither white nor black. I wonder what Ledbetter would think of a Hawaiian or Tongan or Fijian reggae band? I know this may seem odd to many, but ever since Bob Marley passed through the Pacific, reggae music has been a very big thing. Hawaiians and other Pacific Islanders instantly related to Marley's vibe and embraced his music like a long-lost brother.

A local (white) record reviewer dissed the reggae album *Kanakafari* by the Hawaiian band Ho'aikane, calling it "cultural plagiarism" and accusing the band of abandoning their Hawaiian roots and being influenced by a "foreign" culture. I told him that he would have been more comfortable if the album had taken its influence from a European form of Christianity rather than an African one. I wrote that feeling a kinship with Africa was no more a "foreign" influence than the English language that we are all taught in school. Am I (politically or logically) wrong about this?

I would guess that Ledbetter may feel more sympathetic toward Pacific people who feel kinship toward African culture than white people who try to cash in on it. But should all white musicians face exile into the country & western bin? Although many white people live in the smug insulation of their privileged status, many are willing to venture out. Why discourage that?

And finally, what about folks like me? Will I be adjudged deluded and insane, or perhaps just another exploitive cultural pirate? Is there a place in this world for a "Japanee [sic] boy from Hawaii" who surrendered to reggae's calling? H. DOUGHATSUOKA, HONOLULU

What impressed me the most about the first issue of *Vibe* is what seems to be a strong feminist/womanist presence in the articles and philosophies of your writers. I sincerely hope that your magazine makes a strong commitment to criticizing blatantly sexist lyrics and destructive images of male violence in the hip hop industry.

As I grow older and increasingly adopt feminist principles, it's frustrating to find that the male-dominated music I've made a large part of my life is contrary to the ideals of equality and unity that it claims to be fighting for. Now it seems I can no longer tolerate the bitch/ho/golddigger/skeezer lyrics that so many rappers use.

There are many young women out there, like myself, whose values and beliefs are greatly influenced by hip hop. I hope that, unlike other mags, *Vibe* will make a concerted effort to address equally the views and concerns of B-boys and B-girls alike. R.J. HAINES, MONTREAL, QUEBEC

You are to be commended on your preview publication, there is much heart in what *Vibe* promises to become. Except Bönz Malone's "Misda Manners" column. Brother Manners, do take some journalistic responsibility. Some youth might think you're implying that to "boost the flyest shit out of the store" is OK. Aren't the statistics of our black brothers in jail high enough? My brother, when you have such a wonderful opportunity to speak to so many people, be careful what you say, someone might be listening. R. OWINGS, NEW YORK CITY

L.L. Cool J made some outrageous comments in his interview with Kristine McKenna. According to L.L., "Everybody knows that black women are less subject to racism than black men." As proof L.L. cites that "the corporate ladder is filled with black women and white men and women." Meanwhile, black men have "people slamming the door" in their faces.

Please! Just as many doors, if not more, are slammed in black women's faces. If it's not because we're black, then it's because we're women. Sexism combined with racism keeps most black women concentrated on the lower rungs of the corporate ladder doing clerical, entry-level work. Those black women higher up find it difficult to deal with the boys'- club atmosphere that blocks them from obtaining positions of real power. Being black is hard, but white America still places a lot of value on being male. Ask black filmmaker Julie Dash if she can get the kind of money and studio backing that Spike Lee, John Singleton, or the Hudlin brothers get.

Worst of all, we have to fight sexism from our own. How many times have black men referred to us as nothing but bitches and hoes? Rappers are especially at fault in this respect. Before L.L. decides to talk about what "everybody knows" again, he should ask more of everybody. CRYSTAL MARIE SMITH, NEW HAVEN

I didn't like "It's Deep" by Michael Small [Book column] because it was extremely stereotyped. It talks about black people getting hype on the beach and all that white people get is skin cancer. I am white and lived in South Central L.A., until last week. I've been through hell and back. I've gotten shit all over the place just because I'm white. I've had some guy at a restaurant tell my boyfriend (who is black) that he could come in and eat but I couldn't, all because I'm white. I was one of three whites in a Latino gang. When we'd get jumped I would be jumped first and the hardest. It's not all that "great" being white. I'm not saying blacks don't have it hard, I know they do, I'm just saying don't be so quick to judge all white people. If we want things to change, that's not the way to go. AMY TENANT, SEATTLE

DRIVEBY SHOOTING BROOKLYN, NEW YORK ALICE ARNOLD

Magazine Page
Vibe

Designers
Richard Baker
Lee Ellen Fanning

© *Vibe* 1993

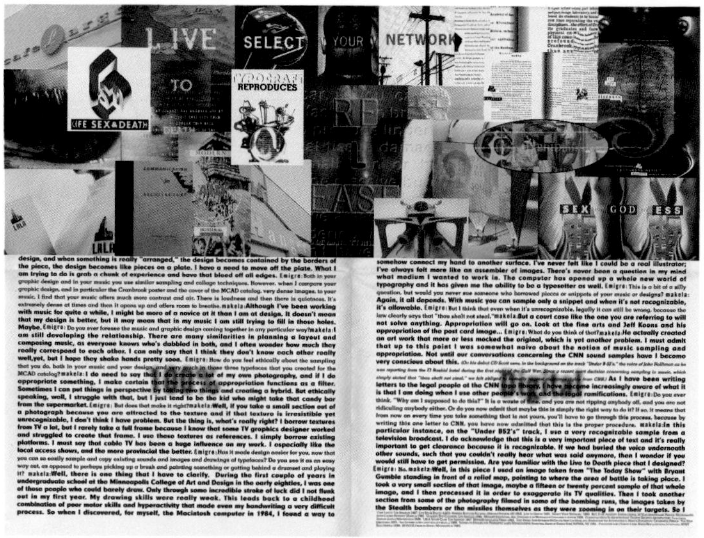

design, and when something is really "arranged," the design becomes contained by the borders of the piece, the design becomes like pieces on a plate. I have a need to move off the plate. What I am trying to do is grab a chunk of experience and have that bleed off all edges. Emigre: Both in your graphic design and in your music you use similar sampling and collage techniques. However, when I compare your graphic design, and in particular the Cranbrook poster and the cover of the MCAD catalog, very dense images, to your music, I find that your music offers much more contrast and air. There is loudness and then there is quietness. It's extremely dense at times and then it opens up and offers room to breathe. makela: Although I've been working with music for quite a while, I might be more of a novice at it than I am at design. It doesn't mean that my design is better, but it may mean that in my music I am still trying to fill in those holes. Maybe. Emigre: Do you ever foresee the music and graphic design coming together in any particular way? makela: I am still developing the relationship. There are many similarities in planning a layout and composing music, as everyone knows who's dabbled in both, and I often wonder how much they really correspond to each other. I can only say that I think they don't know each other really well, yet, but I hope they shake hands pretty soon. Emigre: How do you feel ethically about the sampling that you do, both in your music and your design, and very much in those three typefaces that you created for the MCAD catalog? makela: I do need to say that I do create a lot of my own photography, and if I do appropriate something, I make certain that the process of appropriation functions as a filter. Sometimes I can put things in perspective by taking two things and creating a hybrid. But ethically speaking, well, I struggle with that, but I just tend to be the kid who might take that candy bar from the supermarket. Emigre: But does that make it right? makela: Well, if you take a small section out of a photograph because you are attracted to the texture and if that texture is irresistible yet unrecognizable, I don't think I have problem. But the thing is, what's really right? I borrow textures from TV a lot, but I rarely take a full frame because I know that some TV graphics designer worked and struggled to create that frame. I use those textures as references. I simply borrow existing platforms. I must say that cable TV has been a huge influence on my work. I especially like the local access shows, and the more provincial the better. Emigre: Has it made design easier for you, now that you can so easily sample and copy existing sounds and images and drawings of typefaces? Do you see it as an easy way out, as opposed to perhaps picking up a brush and painting something or getting behind a drumset and playing it? makela: Well, there is one thing that I have to clarify. During the first couple of years in undergraduate school at the Minneapolis College of Art and Design in the early eighties, I was one of those people who could barely draw. Only through some incredible stroke of luck did I not flunk out in my first year. My drawing skills were really weak. This leads back to a childhood combination of poor motor skills and hyperactivity that made even my handwriting a very difficult process. So when I discovered, for myself, the Macintosh computer in 1984, I found a way to somehow connect my hand to another surface. I've never felt like I could be a real illustrator; I've always felt more like an assembler of images. There's never been a question in my mind what medium I wanted to work in. The computer has opened up a whole new world of typography and it has given me the ability to be a typesetter as well. Emigre: This is a bit of a silly question, but would you never sue someone who borrowed pieces or snippets of your music or designs? makela: Again, it all depends. With music you can sample only a snippet and when it's not recognizable, it's allowable. Emigre: But I think that even when it's unrecognizable, legally it can still be wrong, because the law clearly says that "thou shalt not steal." makela: But a court case like the one you are referring to will not solve anything. Appropriation will go on. Look at the fine arts and Jeff Koons and his appropriation of the post card image... Emigre: What do you think of that? makela: He actually created an art work that more or less mocked the original, which is yet another problem. I must admit that up to this point I was somewhat naive about the notion of music sampling and appropriation. Not until our conversations concerning the CNN sound samples have I become very conscious about this. As I have been writing letters to the legal people at the CNN tape library, I have become increasingly aware of what it is that I am doing when I use other people's work and the legal ramifications. Emigre: Do you ever think, "Why am I supposed to do this?" It is a waste of time, and you are not ripping anybody off, and you are not ridiculing anybody either. Or do you now admit that maybe this is simply the right way to do it? If so, it means that from now on every time you take something that is not yours, you'll have to go through this process, because by writing this one letter to CNN, you have now admitted that this is the proper procedure. makela: In this particular instance, on the "Under B52's" track, I use a very recognizable sample from a television broadcast. I do acknowledge that this is a very important piece of text and it's really important to get clearance because it is recognizable. If we had buried the voice underneath other sounds, such that you couldn't really hear what was said anymore, then I wonder if you would still have to get permission. Are you familiar with the Live to Death piece that I designed? Emigre: No. makela: Well, in this piece I used an image taken from "The Today Show" with Bryant Gumble standing in front of a relief map, pointing to where the area of battle is taking place. I took a very small section of that image, maybe a fifteen or twenty percent sample of that whole image, and I then processed it in order to exaggerate its TV qualities. Then I took another section from some of the photography filmed in some of the bombing runs, the images taken by the Stealth bombers or the missiles themselves as they were zooming in on their targets. So I

Poster/Insert
Emigre

Designer
P. Scott Makela

© *P. Scott Makela/Emigre* 1992

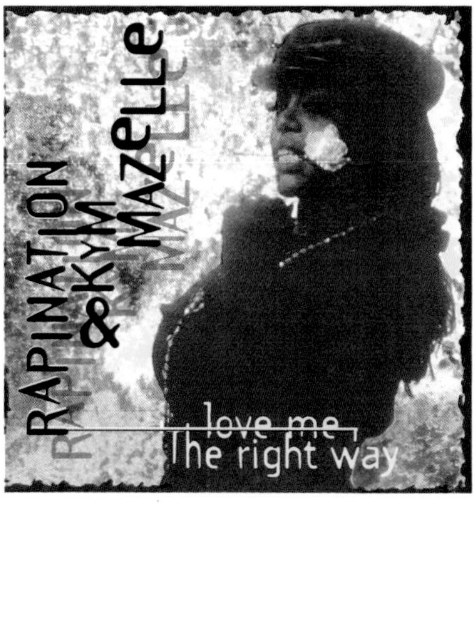

CD Package
Love Me the Right Way

Art Director
Jackie Murphy

Designer
Sean Smith

© *RCA Records* 1993

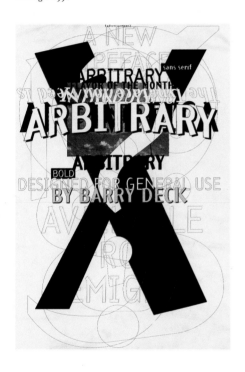

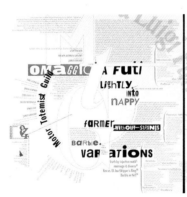

When Gutenberg invented movable type the letterforms he used replicated Germanic scripts. Although his Mainz press would ultimately open the door for additional styles of type to be developed, his greatest contribution was ostensibly to the technology of printing. Similarly, when Apple Inc. introduced the Macintosh computer its creators never dreamed that it would have such a tremendous impact on graphic design, no less typography. The earliest Macs did not have enough memory to create

and store designed layouts. These machines were loaded with default, low resolution bitmapped typefaces that could not compare in quality with existing types. Therefore it took real imagination to understand their potential as a design tool. Within a short time high resolution fonts were put into use, and now thousands are available. But in the interim only a few pioneers attempted to use the roughly hewn faces. Yet thanks to these intrepid souls the Mac became a fount of typographic ingenuity. Making the Mac's limitation into an advantage required a fair amount of play. The machine was more than a serious toy. Making radical bitmapping from the proverbial sow's ear into a silk purse was not easy. But the Mac users determined that smoothing the textures out was not necessarily advantageous, and therefore making silk was not the objective. Nor was Mac lettering a diamond in the rough, but it was the first step in developing typographic norms for the computer. Moreover, Mac type was the basis of a distinct typographic dialect that not only signaled the advent of the age of

computer-aided design but of a period of accelerated typeplay. *Emigre* was the clarion of Mac lettering, and in its earliest incarnation as a culture tabloid on the cusp of becoming an influential design magazine it proved the viable application of bitmapped exaggeration. With so many improvements in the technology, today Mac lettering is less of a statement and more of a style, but that it initially provided designers with usable options cannot be undervalued.

CD/Package
Hard Hip Hop

Designer/Type
Elliott Earls

© *Elektra Entertainment* 1993

BAD LETTERING

I HAVE FOUND, IS USUALLY BEGINS WITH THE PREMISE THAT ALL LETTER **PREDICTABLE.** WIDTHS, LIKE ALL MEN, ARE CREATED EQUAL. THE LAY LETTERER THEN ADDS **THE TYPICAL MISTAKES** SERIFS TO THE "I" SO IT WILL FILL UP ITS **MADE BY LAY LETTERERS** SLOT. THERE IS NO CONSISTENCY TO **OFTEN FOLLOW SIMILAR** THE RADIUSES OF CURVES IN CURVED **LINES. I'VE MARVELLED** CHARACTERS, NOT EVEN WITHIN THE **OVER THIS FOR YEARS. SUCH** SAME CHARACTER. MOST **OBSERVATIONS FORMED THE** PERPLEXING, IS THAT THE **BASIS OF A REALLY LOUSEY** LAY LETTERER MIXES THICK+ **FONT CALLED** THIN STROKES WITH MONO-WEIGHT LETTER FORMS. THEN HE CONFUSES THE ORDER OF THE THICK+THIN **BADTYP.** STROKES OF ROMAN TYPE AS THOUGH HE'D NEVER SEEN A NEWSPAPER IN HIS LIFE OR CAN'T REFER TO ONE.

Set in Cabarga BADTYP

consistency is the hobgoblin of little minds: except in lettering design. Set in Cabarga CYMBAL. 1234567890

Font Specimen
Cabarga BADTYP

Designer
Leslie Cabarga

© *Leslie Cabarga and The Font Bureau* 1993

Logo
Rocky River School District

Designer/Letterer
Nancy Bero Petro

© *Rocky River Board of Education* 1987

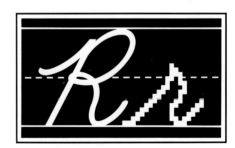

Egiziano Classic Black	Egiziano Classic Black Shadow
ABCDEFG HIJKLMN OPQRSTU VWXYZ(& .,;:'""?!/-*#) abcdefghij klmnopqrs tuvwxyz12 34567890	ABCDEFG HIJKLMN OPQRSTU VWXYZ(& .,;:'""?!/-*#) abcdefghij klmnopqrs tuvwxyz12 34567890
Set at 40 point, minus leaded 2 points	Set at 40 point, minus leaded 2 points

Franklin Gothic Triple Condensed	Franklin Gothic Wide
ABCDEFGHIJKLMN OPQRSTUVWXYZ(& .,;:'""?!/-*#)abcd efghijklmnopqrstu vwxyz1234567890	ABCDEFG HIJKLMN OPQRSTU VWXYZ(& .,;:'""?!/-*#) abcdefghij klmnopqrs tuvwxyz12 34567890
Set at 40 point, minus leaded 2 points. An original design	Set at 40 point, minus leaded 2 points.

Font Catalog
A Great Collection
Designer
Dennis Ortiz-Lopez
© *Dennis Ortiz-Lopez* 1990-93

O-L Hebrew Graphic Script with Nikkud

אבגדההוזחחטי"

Designed for use in Adobe Illustrator
without the hebrew finder, this font features
a complete set of vowels, hard and soft
consonants and hebraic sorts

כללמנסעפצ

קרששתדסמוּפץ:

**THIS FONT MAY ALSO BE ORDERED FROM FONTHAUS
WITHOUT TECHNICAL SUPPORT**

O-L Hebrew Deco

אבגדההוזחחשי

A four-layered titling font designed
for use in Adobe Illustrator without the
hebrew finder. Consonants only

כללמנסעפצ

קרששתדסמוּפ:ץ

A B C D

GOOD LETTERING *requires as much skill as good painting or good sculpture.*

E F G H I

Although it serves a definite purpose and not necessarily eternity, good lettering

J K L M

is equal to the fine arts. The designer of letters, whether he be a sign painter, a

N O P Q R

graphic artist or in the service of a type foundry, participates just as creatively

S T U V

in shaping the style of his time as the architect or poet. – JAN TSCHICHOLD

W X Y Z

Font Specimen
S.I. Gothic
Designer
Jonathan Hoefler
© *The Hoefler Type Foundry* 1991

Font Specimen
Egiziano Classic
Designer
Jonathan Hoefler
© *The Hoefler Type Foundry* 1991

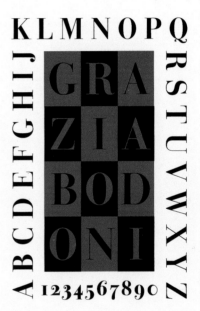

83

Font Specimen
Grazia Bodoni
Designer
Jonathan Hoefler
© *The Hoefler Type Foundry* 1991

BEHOLD
S. I. FEATHERWEIGHT
SIX EXCITING NEW
S. I. LIGHTWEIGHT
FACES
S. I. HEAVYWEIGHT
DEVELOPED ESPECIALLY
S. I. MIDDLEWEIGHT
FOR SPORTS
S. I. WELTERWEIGHT
ILLUSTRATED
S. I. BANTAMWEIGHT

Chapter 8

N

ot unlike a visual pun, which is an image that has two or more meanings, the metamorphosis of type and letters is the transformation of a conventional form into another object or image. Graphic design puns are most commonly achieved through the metamorphosis of a letterform into something that is other than its original form, while at the same time it still reads as the letterform. Using hot metal typecase letters the Russian Constructivists arduously transformed letters into human figurations by carefully jumbling the letters so that they still read as a word but also revealed a pictograph or character. In his book of *Calligrames*, the French Surrealist poet Apollinaire metamorphosed words in a poem about rain into the rain itself by composing them vertically down the page, not unlike the naive manner of a child when toying with writing at an early developmental stage. In a prefiguration of Surrealism, the English writer Lewis Carroll in *Through the Looking-Glass* metamorphosed a piece of type into the shape of a mouse's tail to allow the reader the added experience of seeing as well as reading (and hearing) his fantastic tale. Of all the tools for play at the designer's disposal the metamorphosis of type is one of the most difficult, for the result could easily be two-thirds of a pun, as one used to say in elementary school, if it is not smartly done. Yet when successful, metamorphosed type is also one of the most satisfying because it is the quintessential designer's game. The joy derived from realizing and solving the metamorphic puzzle adds greatly to the reader/viewer experience. Which, incidentally, addresses the paramount issue in graphic design—to grab and hold attention.

META
MO
8
PHIC

Book Jacket
Lust

Art Director
Sara Eiseman

Designer
Carin Goldberg

© *Houghton Mifflin* 1988

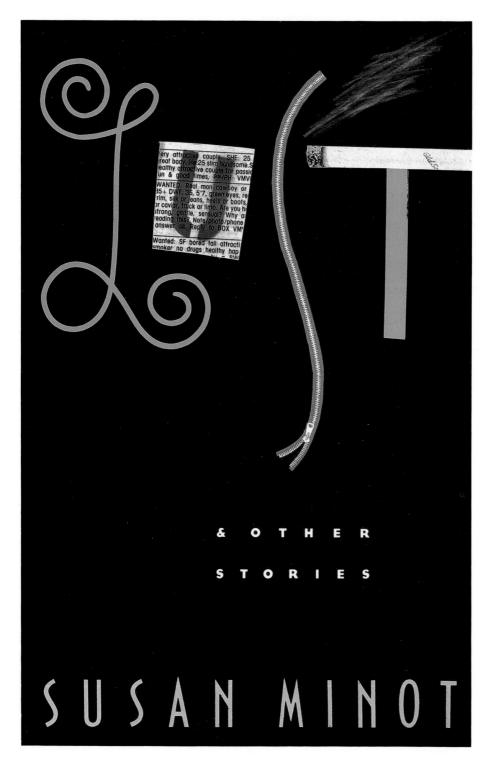

HEAT
WAVE

Logo
Bloomingdale's Summer
Campaign

Creative Director
John Jay

Designer/Typography
Tim Girvin

© *Tim Girvin Design, Inc.* 1985

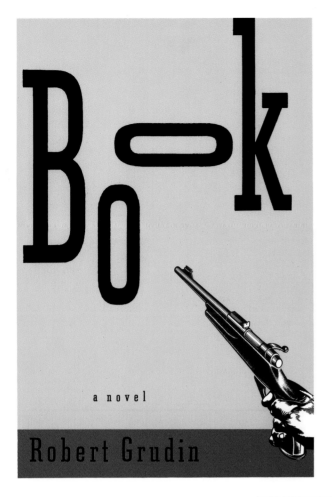

Book Jacket
Book

Designer
Archie Ferguson

Illustrator
Mark Falls

© *Random House, Inc.* 1992

Logotype
Sun Microsystems

Art Director/Designer
Earl Gee

© *Earl Gee Design* 1991

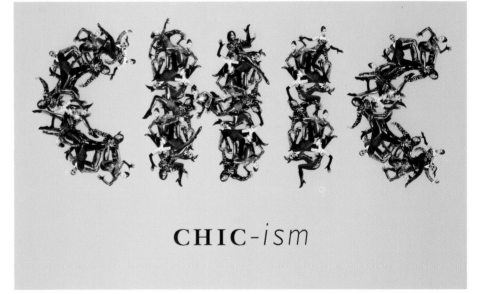

CHIC-*ism*

Poster
Chic-ism

Art Directors
Robin Lynch
Jeff Gold

Designer
Robin Lynch

Photographer
Stephan Sednaoui

© *Warner Bros. Records* 1992

Newspaper Pages
The New York Times

Art Director
Mirko Ilic

Designers
Sam Reep *left*
Gary Cosimini *right*

Illustrators
Milan Trenc *left*

© *The New York Times* 1992

Newspaper Pages
The New York Times

Art Director
Mirko Ilic

Designers
Mirko Ilic *left*
Sam Reep *right*

Illustrators
Alejandro Arce *left*
Ruth Marten *right*

© *The New York Times* 1992

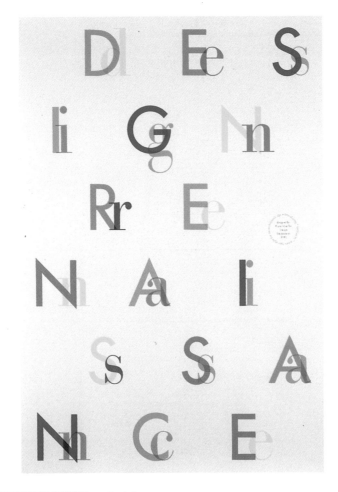

Poster
Design Renaissance

Art Director
Paula Scher

Designers
Ron Louie
Paula Scher

© *Pentagram* 1993

Book Cover
Real Estate

Designer
Paula Scher

© *Simon & Schuster* 1988

Poster
Dallas Art Directors Club

Art Director/Designer
Paula Scher

© *Pentagram* 1992

Movie Logo
Rites of Summer

Designer
FRANKFURT GIPS BALKIND
Peter Nguyen

© *Peter Nguyen* 1988

Logo
Daven Film & Video

Designer
Earl Gee

© *Earl Gee Design* 1991

Poster
SPD Call for Entries

Art Director
Fred Woodward

Designers
Fred Woodward
Gail Anderson

Illustrators
Terry Allen
Dennis Ortiz-Lopez

© *Society of Publication Designers* 1990

GEEK LOVE

A NOVEL

KATHERINE DUNN

Book Jacket
Geek Love
Designer
Chip Kidd
© *Chip Kidd* 1989

BIG SHOTS

Movie Logo
Big Shots
Designer
FRANKFURT GIPS BALKIND
Peter Nguyen
© *Peter Nguyen* 1987

Self-Promotional Piece
Bon Appetit!

Designers
Bernard Maisner
Nora Scarlett

Letterer
Bernard Maisner

Photographer
Nora Scarlett

© *Maisner & Scarlett* 1992

93

Newspaper Page
The Wall Street Journal

Art Director/Designer
Greg Leeds

Illustrator
David Suter

© *Dow Jones & Co., Inc.* 1990

Chapter 9

From out of the foam of the current wave of complexity comes a new approach to old typography. As a response, indeed a reaction, to the chaotic activity that has come to signify contemporary typeplay, the reappreciation of simple classical methods is gaining new adherents. The New Classicism is not a movement or fashion—by no means is it a new wave—but it does suggest a new sobriety in the wake of what some have criticized as the wanton antics of Post-Modernism. Rather than an ideology based on fundamental strictures, The New Classicism is an alternative form of play. Only this time rather than an experiment with the unknown and untested it is a reconfiguration of the tried and true. And yet this is not a nostalgic approach that desperately recalls the "good ole days," but instead classic types are being reappreciated in decidedly contemporary compositions that derive from, but are not overly influenced by, the latest technologies. The idea that type can be recast in the manner of hot metal has been rejected for the here and now. But that does not mean that typography must be slavishly wed to fashion, either. The New Classicism is being practiced by those who respect the past, but understand the present communications environment. It is also the playing field for those who have seriously toyed with the new wave but ultimately were stymied by the inherent limitations found in its stylistic trappings. The New Classicism is concerned with reducing complexity, focusing on the essentials, and returning to more accessible composition. This implies both a return to the traditional central axis and Modernist ornament-free approaches. But even though the New Classicism is a confluence of these two aesthetics it is not locked into one or the other. The result is often a pleasing, indeed refined, typography that respects the word as meaning (the cornerstone of communication), not as texture.

THE NEW
CLASSICISM

Me

Stories of My Life

Katharine Hepburn

Book Jacket
White People

Designer
Chip Kidd

© *Alfred A. Knopf* 1990

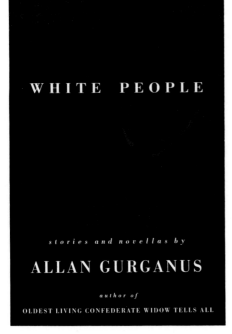

WHITE PEOPLE

stories and novellas by

ALLAN GURGANUS

author of

OLDEST LIVING CONFEDERATE WIDOW TELLS ALL

96

Book Jacket
Me

Designers
Chip Kidd
Carol Devine Carson

© *Alfred A. Knopf* 1991

Logo
General Contractors
Inspection Service
Designer
Bruce Yelaska

© *Bruce Yelaska* 1989

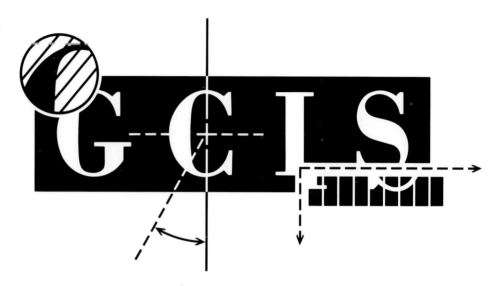

Album Cover
Brahms/Mozart
Art Director
Bob Hurwitz
Designer
Carin Goldberg

© *Nonesuch Records* 1985

BRAHMS

CLARINET QUINTET IN B MINOR, OP. 115

MOZART

CLARINET QUINTET IN B-FLAT MAJOR, K. ANH. 91/516C

SEQUOIA STRING

QUARTET

WITH

MICHELE ZUKOVSKY

CLARINET

Magazine Spread
Rolling Stone

Art Director/Designer
Fred Woodward

Letterer
Anita Karl

Photographer
Albert Watson

© *Wenner Media, Inc.* 1992

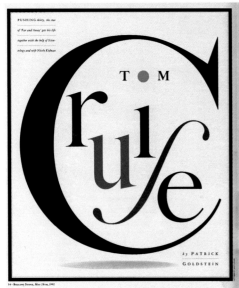

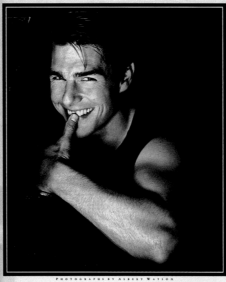

Magazine Spread
Rolling Stone

Art Director/Designer
Fred Woodward

Photographer
Albert Watson

© *Wenner Media, Inc.* 1990

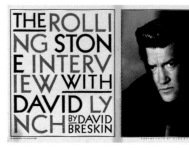

98

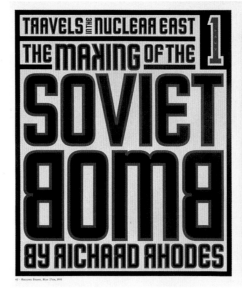

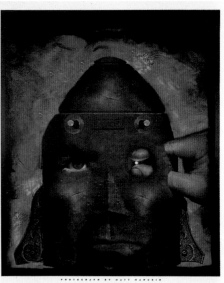

Magazine Spread
Rolling Stone

Art Director
Fred Woodward

Designer
Gail Anderson

Photographer
Matt Mahurin

© *Wenner Media, Inc.* 1993

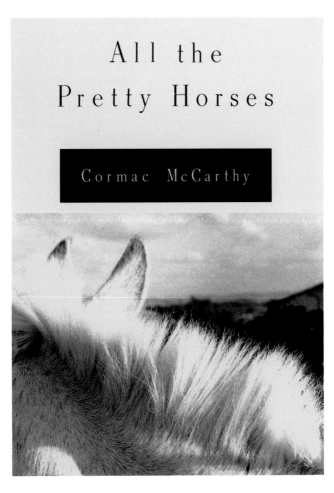

Book Cover
Genesis and Exodus

Designer
Archie Ferguson

© *Pantheon Books* 1991

Book Jacket
All the Pretty Horses

Designer
Chip Kidd

Photographer
David Katzenstein

© *Chip Kidd* 1992

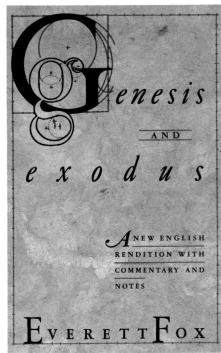

Book Jacket
Ever After

Art Director/Designer
Carol Devine Carson

© *Alfred A. Knopf* 1992

Book Jacket
In the Form of a Person

Art Director
Carol Devine Carson

Designer
Barbara de Wilde

Photographer
Paul Schuitema

© *Barbara de Wilde* 1992

in the form of a person ann pyne

Annual Report
Collagen Corporation

Designers
Earl Gee
Fani Chung

Photographer
Geoffrey Nelson

© *Earl Gee Design* 1992

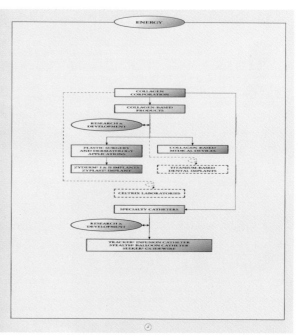

Magazine Page
Rolling Stone

Art Director
Fred Woodward

Designer
Debra Bishop

Letterer
Anita Karl

© *Wenner Media, Inc.* 1992

Book Jacket
A Writer's Life
Designer
Louise Fili
© *Louise Fili* 1993

Logo
Del Bosque
Designers
Chris Hill
Jeff Davis
© *Chris Hill/A Marketing Group* 1992

DEL BOSQUE

IOI

Book Jacket
The Queen's Throat
Art Director
Frank Metz
Designer
Carin Goldberg
© *Simon & Schuster* 1993

The
QUEEN'S
THROAT
· OPERA ·
Homo
SEXUALITY
and the
MYSTERY
of
· DESIRE ·
· WAYNE ·
KOESTENBAUM

The Macintosh has become a tool, if not a platform, for a rash of new typefaces. The word *font,* once used only by printers and graphic designers, has come into common usage. Like other technical words and phrases that have been adopted into the vernacular, *font* will be with us for a long time. Font packages are currently available as common peripherals to anyone who works a PC. The once improbable idea that everyone will own a personal typeface is actually coming true. If printing was considered a democratic art when only a few people had access to a printing press, and even fewer could run them, what is it now that everyone has access to a PC, laser printer, and even more importantly, type. Like the telephone, the personal computer has become a standard communications medium, and type has emerged as its common voice. It was in the early stages of this environment that timidly at first a few intrepid type designers switched from designing for film over to digital media. Now even designers who would have never thought to call themselves typographers have begun designing customized faces. The availability of type design programs has made it seem that anyone with programmatic skills can achieve the same results as type designers. And while on occasion the neophyte might by chance design a few interesting display letters, the odds of creating a viable alphabet remain slim. The best custom display faces are still those rendered by skilled designers, who have a sense of how the letters will perform in context and when they converge with other forms. But most important, viable text alphabets must still be administered by those skilled artisans who can wed legibility and aesthetics. The New Faces that are being issued on a regular basis cannot be judged by who designed them (even good designers design bad faces), but the odds are that the most effective are created by skilled designers who understand the nuances of type.

new

FACES

Typeface Specimen
Motion
Designer
Frank Heine
© *Emigre* 1993

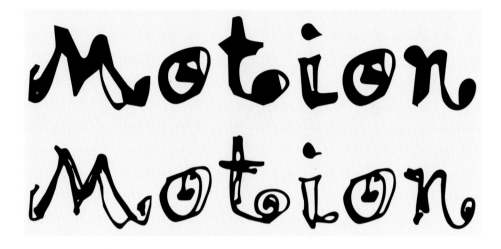

Typeface Specimen
Oakland Ten
Designer
Zuzana Licko
© *Emigre* 1986

104

Typeface Specimen
Missionary
Designer
Miles Newlyn
© *Emigre* 1993

ORIGINAL TYPEFACES
Designed by Barry Deck

Barry Sans Serif
ABCDEFGHIJKLMNOPQRSTUVWXYZ
abcdefghijklmnopqrstuvwxyz
1234567890

Canicopulis Script
ABCDEFGHIJKLMNOPQRSTUVWXYZ
abcdefghijklmnopqrstuvwxyz
1231567890

CAUSTIC BIOMORPH EXTRA BOLD
ABCDEFGHIJKLMNO
PQRSTUVWXYZ
1234567890

Washed Out Plenty
ABCDEFGHIJKLMNOPQRSTUVWXYZ
abcdefghijklmnopqrstuvwxyz
1234567890

PORTFOLIO
TIME & EFFORT CO. | for all your TYPOGRAPHICAL NEEDS! call (718)832-5644

Portfolio Page
Original Typefaces
Designer
Barry Deck
© *Barry Deck* 1992

Typeface Specimen
Template Gothic
Designer
Barry Deck
© *Emigre* 1991

Template Gothic

⚘·LIBRIS·⚘
BY JONATHAN MACAGBA

BASED ON THE LETTERING OF AN EARLY
TWELFTH CENTURY SPANISH MANUSCRIPT

≈ AABCCDEFGHH ≈
IJKLMMNOOPPQRS
TUVVWWXYZ&
≈ 1234567890 LEFI ≈

NOW AVAILABLE FOR THE MACINTOSH OR WINDOWS
TYPE-1 & TRUETYPE VERSIONS INCLUDED

≈ $35 POSTPAID
PA RES. ADD 7%

TO ORDER, CONTACT YOUR DEALER OR ORDER DIRECTLY FROM:
HANDCRAFTEDFONTS CO. ✥ P.O. BOX 14013 ✥ PHILA. PA 19122 ✥ TELEPHONE (215) 634·0634

Font Specimen
Cabarga Kobalt
Cabarga Progressiv

Designer
Leslie Cabarga

*© Kobalt™ Leslie Cabarga
and The Font Bureau* 1993

—F. G. Cooper, c. 1930
"LETTERING
struck an awful snag
in the river of time when printing was invented.
TYPOGRAPHY
tends to establish letterforms
frozen in tradition.
& limited by its mechanical medium."

Set in Cabarga Kobalt

COMPUTER TYPE
blurs the line between hand lettering and type.
In the past, the technical expertise required to
render quality lettering left out all but a few.
The computer has obviated much of the drawing, measuring and inking associated with traditional lettering but it cannot produce correct
letterforms or a feeling for letter design.
The computer-generated wave
which the novice letterer rides to compe-
tence also propels the expert that much farther.

Set in Cabarga PROGRESSIV

106

HE & SHE

Many writers feel uncomfortable using the masculine pronoun when
referring to a person of either gender. But recasting a sentence to
eliminate male pronouns is sometimes difficult or undesirable. It may seem
awkward to use both masculine and feminine pronouns (as in "When the
commuter arrives at the station he or she often finds the train late.").
Use of the feminine pronoun alone, as the male is used,
may raise questions in readers' minds as to whether the object of
the sentence is a "she" specifically.
In order to establish a balance of terms when referring to people
generally, when no specific sex is indicated, I have developed a system of
replacement pronouns described below.

She and he become **she** (pronounced suh-he)
His and hers become **hiers** (pronounced hears)
Her and him become **herin** (pronounced hurin)
Man, becomes **man** (pronounced wuh-man)

Now, when a writer speaks of mankind in general she need not worry that
hiers statement will come back to haunt herin.

Set in Cabarga Ojaio Light   Font includes the ligatures sh & fh

Typeface Specimen
Libris Light

Designer
Jonathan Macagba

Foundry
Handcraftedfonts Company

© Jonathan Macagba 1993

Font Specimen
He & She Cabarga Ojaio

Designer
Leslie Cabarga

© Leslie Cabarga 1993

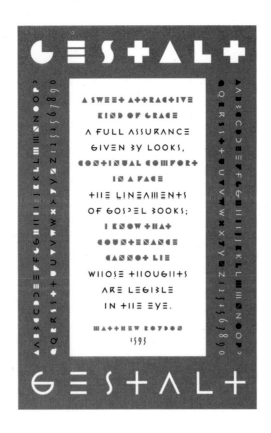

Font Specimen
Hoefler Text Roman

Designer
Jonathan Hoefler

o The Hoefler Type Foundry 1991

Font Specimen
Gestalt

Designer
Jonathan Hoefler

o The Hoefler Type Foundry 1991

HOEFLER TEXT ROMAN

72 POINT

Manifestos

48 POINT

Victorian Poster

36 POINT

Enlightened Republic

28 POINT

Wodehouse Story Published

24 POINT

Amalgamated Industries Report

18 POINT

Science provides the modern designer with

14 POINT

When scuba diving off the coral reefs around St. Kitts, he discovered the most remarkable thing. The sunken

12 POINT

Often the Manx deposited itself neatly in front of their Trinitron

10 POINT

The theater's construction was such that it sadly afforded a full view of the show to all but the luckiest patrons

9 POINT

The neighbors all gathered to mourn the passing of dear Agatha, dead at 91 rest her soul, and express their deep concern for the welfare of her old, spacious apartment

7 POINT

Seasoned fishermen are familiar with a variety of shiny lures and the fish they attract. A spinner will often bring bass; pickerel will respond to a black fury fly. The intrepid angler is wont to cast a line with his companions' car keys, for hours of play

CHARACTERS IN COMPLETE FONT

A B C D E F G H I J K L M
N O P Q R S T U V W X Y Z
a b c d e f g h i j k l m n o p q r
s t u v w x y z 1 2 3 4 5 6 7 8 9 0
Å Á À Â Ä Ã å á à â ä ã Ç ç É È
Ê Ë é è ê ë Í Ì Î Ï í ì î ï Ñ ñ Ø
Ó Ò Ô Ö Õ ø ó ò ô ö õ Ú Ù Û
Ü ú ù û ü Ÿ ÿ … . , : ; „ ‚ " " ' ' ' '
^ ` ˜ ¯ ˘ ˙ ¨ ˚ ˝ ˛ ˇ ‹ › « » < > [ ] ( ) { }
/ | \ - – — = ÷ + ± _ ? ¿ ! ¡ & * ° @ #
% ‰ $ ¢ £ ¥ ƒ © ® ™ ª º · • ¶ §
† ‡ Æ æ Œ œ ß fi fl ff ffi ffl ☞

XAVIER

ABCDEF GHIJKL MNOPQ RSTUV WXY&Z

AN ORIGINAL
DESIGN BY JASON CASTLE

Font Specimen
Xavier

Designer
Jason Castle

© *Jason Castle* 1992-93

ABCDE
FGHIJK
LMNOP
QRSTU
VWXYZ

34

abcdef
ghijklm
nopqrst
uvwxyz
&åçéĝñ

35

ABCDE
FGHIJK
LMNOP
QRSTUV
WXYZ
(+.,!!?!"
/12345
67890)

Typeface Specimen
Bloodstream
Designers
SMOKEBOMB STUDIO
Nancy Mazzei, Brian Kelly
© *Smokebomb Studio* 1993

Font Catalog
A Great Collection
Designer
Dennis Ortiz-Lopez
© *Dennis Ortiz-Lopez* 1990-93

Chapter 11

Nostalgia was once a disease. "Nostalgia, neuralgia, take a bromo and call me in the morning." Actually, in the sixteenth century the nausea and heartburn felt by young soldiers and caused by melancholy and homesickness during wartime was a very serious malady. Today nostalgia, the longing for yesterday, is more a mental (dis)order that affects people who sometimes have never even lived through the particular period that they are nostalgic for. Playing on this passion for the past has made nostalgia, the appropriation of old styles, into a common marketing tool for businesses and their advertising agencies. In graphic design and typography the past has become a viable and ubiquitous plaything. Nostalgia is at best a serious reapplication of historical material, and at worst a flagrant sampling of decontextualized forms, but it is definitely a significant mediator in contemporary practice. The past offers a toy chest of scrap from which designers can select the equivalent of costumes for dress up. Some religiously adhere to the historical models, and the verisimilitude of various Victorian, Art Nouveau, Art Deco, and Constructivist design makes it almost impossible to distinguish between the real and phony. Others use the past as a springboard to new discoveries. In the 1960s Push Pin Studios reprised Art Moderne (a.k.a. Art Deco) as "The Roxy Style," a hybrid of 1920s/30s decoration and sixties colors. In the 1980s Paula Scher recalled 1920s Russian Constructivism as an eclectic way of reintroducing viable design approaches considered passé or forgotten. And other designers simply return to the past (as presented in design annuals and magazines) for inspiration, borrowing or sampling bits and pieces for contemporary design. Much of the typographic nostalgia today focuses on the artifacts of commercial culture that have been made musty by time, but are charming by virtue of their age. Like playing with old toys encrusted with comparative innocence, toying with old types designed for comparatively more naive purposes will always have appeal.

NOSTALGIA

Book Jacket
The Lost Book of Paradise

Art Director
Victor Weaver

Designer
Carin Goldberg

Illustrator
Barbara Nessim

© *Hyperion Books* 1993

Book Cover
Ulysses

Art Director
Judith Loeser

Designer
Carin Goldberg

© *Vintage Books* 1986

Album Cover
Dvořák: Smetana

Art Director
Bob Hurwitz

Designer
Carin Goldberg

© *Nonesuch Records* 1986

Beer Label
Gorky's

Designers
Henry Vizcarra
Estay Heustis

© *Gorky's Russian Brewery* 1991

Book Jacket
The Divine Sarah

Designer
Louise Fili

© *Alfred A. Knopf* 1992

113

CD Package
The Very Very Best of
Dorsey Burnette

Art Director/Designer
Randall Martin

Illustrator
Peter Castro

© *Chrysalis Music
Group Inc.* 1991

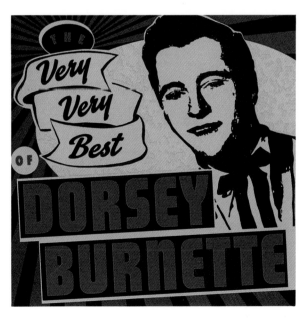

Poster
AIGA/SF
Designer
Earl Gee
© *Earl Gee Design* 1990

Book Cover
The Gaga Years
Designer
Helene Silverman
© *Carol Publishing Group* 1992

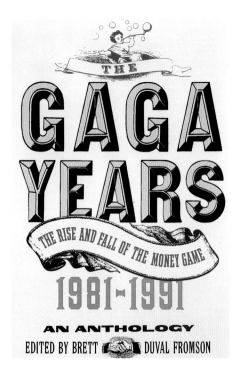

114

Logo
Mudhoney
Designer
Art Chantry
© *Art Chantry* 1991

Magazine Spread
Rolling Stone
Art Director
Fred Woodward
Designer
Debra Bishop
Letterer
Anita Karl
Photographer
Kurt Marcus
© *Wenner Media, Inc.* 1990

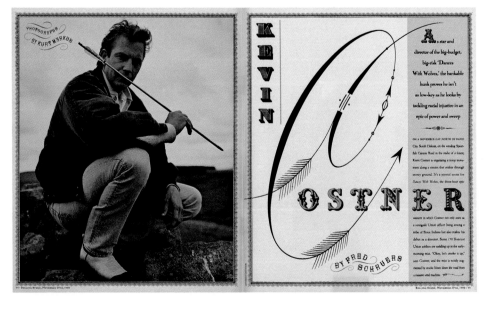

Subway Poster
The S.S. Dragnet

Designers
Drew Hodges
Peter Mackey

© *Nickelodeon* 1991

Book Cover
Italian Art Deco

Art Director/Designer
Louise Fili

Typeface Designer
Jonathan Hoefler

© *Louise Fili* 1993

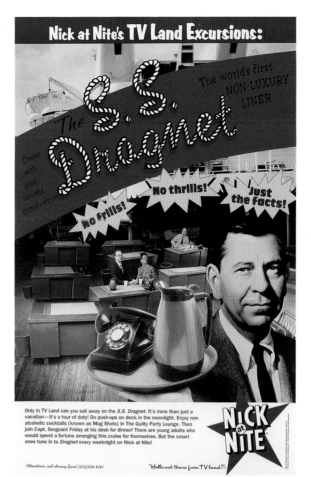

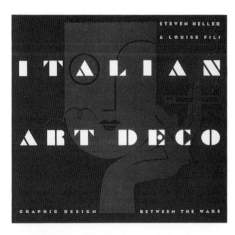

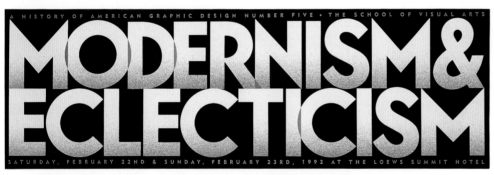

Poster
Modernism & Eclecticism

Art Director/Designer
Louise Fili

© *Louise Fili* 1992

Book Jacket
The Actual Adventures of
Michael Missing

Designer
Chip Kidd

Illustrator
Charles Burns

© *Chip Kidd* 1989

Book Cover
Pricing & Ethical Guidelines
Designer
Daniel Pelavin
© *Daniel Pelavin* 1991

Magazine Cover
Crossover Dreams
Designer
Daniel Pelavin
© *Daniel Pelavin* 1989

Album Cover
Showtime!
Designer
Carin Goldberg
© *EMI Records* 1982

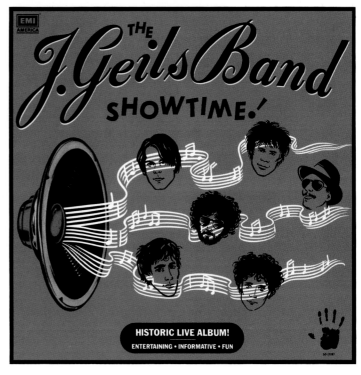

Poster
Bard

Art Director
Paula Scher

Designer
Ron Louie

© *Pentagram* 1992

Book Jacket
Family Values

Art Director
Frank Metz

Designer
Carin Goldberg

Illustrator
Ruth Steed

© *Simon & Schuster* 1993

Magazine Cover
Metropolis

Designers
Helene Silverman
Jeff Christensen

© *Metropolis* 1988

Book Jacket
King of the Wa-Kikuyu

Art Director
Henry Sene Yee

Designer
Angela Skouras

© *St. Martin's Press* 1993

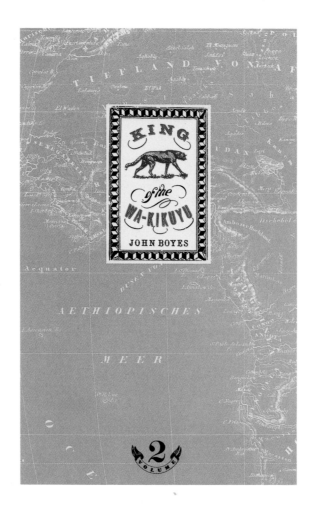

Book Jacket
English Country House Murders

Designer
Miriam Campiz

© *Mysterious Press* 1990

CD Package
Crossfire

Art Directors
Ria Lewerke
Jackie Murphy

Designer
Sean Smith

Photographer
Maryellen McGrath

© *BMG Music and
Reunion Records* 1983

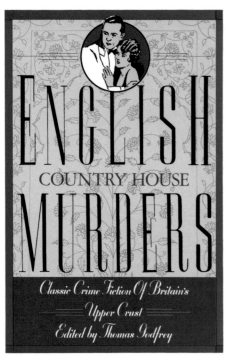

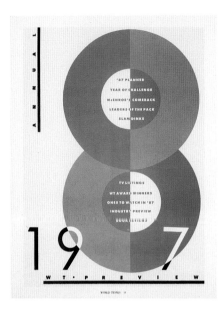

Magazine Page
World Tennis

Designer
Miriam Campiz

© *Media/World Tennis* 1987

Newspaper Page
The Wall Street Journal

Art Director/Designer
Greg Leeds

Illustrator
Mick Wiggins

© *Dow Jones & Co., Inc.* 1990

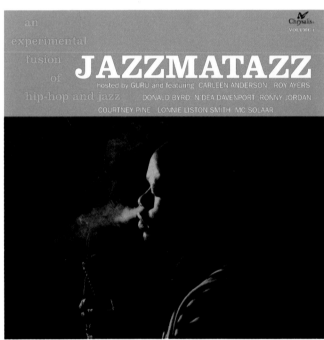

Album Cover
Jazzmatazz

Art Director
Henry Marquez

Designer
Diane Cuddy

Photographer
Humphry Studio

© *EMI Records Group* 1993

Book Jacket
Luncheon at the
Cafe Ridiculous

Art Director
Frank Metz

Designer
Carln Goldberg

Illustrator
Gene Greif

© *Simon & Schuster* 1988

Poster
Zeke Clements

Art Director
Charles S. Anderson

Designer
HATCH SHOW PRINT

© *Charles S. Anderson*
Design Company 1992

Poster
Nike 180 Air

Art Director
Charles S. Anderson

Designers
Daniel Olson
Charles S. Anderson

Illustrators
JAPAN Takenobu Igarashi
GERMANY Alfons Holtgreve
ENGLAND Ralph Steadman
FRANCE Andre Francois
BRAZIL Philipe Taborda

© *Charles S. Anderson*
Design Company 1990

Poster
Nike 180 "A" Air

Art Director
Charles S. Anderson

Designers
Daniel Olson
Charles S. Anderson

Illustrators
JAPAN Takenobu Igarashi
GERMANY Alfons Holtgreve
ENGLAND Ralph Steadman
FRANCE Andre Francois
BRAZIL Philipe Taborda

© *Charles S. Anderson*
Design Company 1990

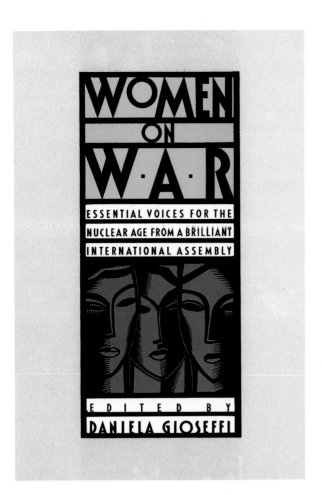

Poster
Cult

Designer
Hugh Brown

© *ArtRock–San Francisco, CA* 1986

Book Jacket
Women on War

Art Director
Frank Metz

Designer
Carin Goldberg

Illustrator
Anthony Russo

© *Simon & Schuster* 1988

Newspaper Page
The Wall Street Journal

Art Director/Designer
Greg Leeds

Illustrator
Wendy Wray

© *Dow Jones & Co., Inc.* 1991

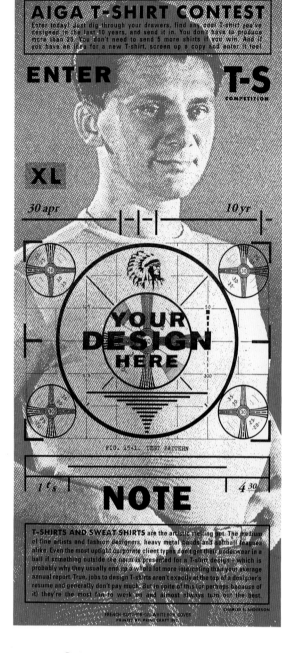

Poster
Dallas Texas

Art Director
Charles S. Anderson

Designers
Charles S. Anderson
Daniel Olson
Todd Hauswirth

© *Charles S. Anderson*
Design Company 1991

122

Poster
C.S.A. Line Art Archive

Art Director
Charles S. Anderson

Designers
Charles S. Anderson
Todd Hauswirth
Daniel Olson

Illustrators
Charles S. Anderson
Randall Dahlk

© *Charles S. Anderson*
Design Company 1992

Poster
AIGA T-Shirt Contest

Art Director
Charles S. Anderson

Designers
Charles S. Anderson
Todd Hauswirth

© *Charles S. Anderson*
Design Company 1992

Invitation
Type 90

Designer
Jonathan Hoefler

© *The Hoefler Type*
Foundry, Inc. 1990

☞ LECTURES

The core of Type90 will be a series of lectures and specialized 'town meetings,' short presentations followed by open discussions. There will be discussions of type history (including James Mosley's examination of antique ornamented types and John Dreyfus' chronicle of Charles Peignot), a look at the type of today (with presentations by post-post modernists Neville Brody and Zuzana Lícko), and some predictions for the type of tomorrow (including Rene Kerfante and Günter Gerhard Lange on the future of type in Europe). Alan Jeeps of the BBC and Frans Lasès will discuss screen type in "The Good Morning Type Show," and Steven Heller will be leading an informal encounter group on "Truly Disgusting Novelty Faces and How to Use Them." Additional presentations will include typeface protection, type marketing for designers and foundries, and type education.

& TOWN MEETINGS

OXFORD

Home to the English-speaking world's oldest university, the "City of Dreaming Spires" is an intellectual paradise. With more than 900 buildings of historical and architectural importance within one square mile, Oxford's streets, houses, colleges and chapels (enhanced by gardens, croquet lawns and shaded, tree-lined walks) showcase centuries of English history. There is no one building that dominates Oxford, no famous fortress or cathedral that offers a short-cut view of the city. The best way to get a feel for Oxford is to spend time wandering through the town, slowly taking it all in.

Type90 has arranged for rooms and meals at the colleges of Christ Church and Corpus Christi, located in central Oxford and near almost all Type90 events. For the best choice of housing, please fill out the reservation card as soon as possible, as hotel space will be extremely limited. PanAm has arranged competitive fares for Type90 attendees. To reach them in the U.S., call (800) 635-8470. Our conference code is CVN10005. Parking in Oxford is extremely limited; British Rail from London's Paddington Station and coach service from Heathrow Airport are quite suitable.

Type90 conferees are doers in real life, and a passive conference isn't what they want. Supplementing the lectures and town meetings will be a collection of workshops, offering an opportunity to be involved, to talk, and to explore in a more relaxed, social setting. Workshops will include "Type Design: The Master Class", Matthew Carter's celebrated workshop from Type 1987, featuring presentations by Sumner Stone, Günter Gerhard Lange and Gerard Unger. Paula Scher and Louise Fili will lead workshops on developing a personal design style with type, and Ronn Campisi and Aurobind Patel will open a discussion of type in publication design. Jim Parkinson will lead a workshop on logotype design, and Jonathan Hoefler will work with participants using type design tools for the Macintosh. John Benson, Lida Lopes Cardozo and David Kindersley will lead stone-cutting workshops, and John Downer will head a workshop on gold leaf signpainting. ¶ For the type-minded explorer, Type90 will include two playrooms stocked with every new tool for type design, typography and desktop publishing you care to get your hands on.

A T Y P I
The *Association Typographique Internationale* Presents

TYPE 90

WE ARE AT AN IMPORTANT JUNCTURE in the history of type. Traditionally the domain of publishers, type is rapidly becoming a tool for everyone. ☞ A world conference, Type90, has been called this summer in Oxford to look at the issues from every possible angle, from aesthetic to technical to legal to lighthearted. ☞ For four days starting August 31, a whirlwind program of workshops, lectures, seminars and typographic events will be attended by an international panel of typophiles, from eminent type designers Matthew Carter and Adrian Frutiger, to leading graphic designers Neville Brody and Paula Scher, to type historians John Dreyfus and James Mosley, to typographic innovators Peter Karow and Rene Kerfante. ☞ In all, almost one hundred major typographers and designers have been invited to present their work, demonstrate techniques, and steer discussion. Type90 promises to be a truly unforgettable event. ☞

CD Package
Shut Up!

Designer
Art Chantry

Photographer
A. Patrick Adams

© *Art Chantry* 1993

Album Cover
Everyday Is a Holiday!

Designer
Art Chantry

© *Art Chantry* 1990

124

Album Cover
Clean as a Broke Dick Dog

Designer
Art Chantry

Photographer
Charles Peterson

© *Art Chantry/Sub Pop Records* 1992

Album Cover
Ritual Dimension of
Sound

Designer
Art Chantry

Photographer
Scott Lindgren, "Coop"

© *Art Chantry/Estrus
Recording Institute* 1992

Logo
The Big Life

Designer
STUDIO SEIREENI
Romane Cameron

Illustrator
Tim Clark

© *Daiei Corporation* 1992

THE DICK VAN DYKE SHOW

There are those who have called
The Dick Van Dyke Show the
best sitcom ever made. And it's
hard to argue with them. Carl
Reiner put together a program
that defied all the rules of its
era. He made Rob Petrie a real
person with a real job that was
integral to the story lines. He
gave Rob and Laura a real marriage between equals, giving
this ultimate classic the texture
of real life. And then he put
together one of the most solid
ensembles ever. Mary Tyler
Moore in her first comic role,
Rose Marie, Morey Amsterdam,
Jerry Paris, and, of course, our
own Chairman, Dick Van Dyke.

The Mary Tyler Moore Show

And then there are those who say that this
is the best sitcom ever. Again, it's hard to argue. The Mary Tyler Moore
Show learned its lessons well from its classic predecessor and became a classic
itself. Mary, Lou, Murray, Ted, Rhoda, Phyllis - those aren't characters. They're our
friends. They're real people. And the things that happen to Mary - with parents, jobs,
neighbors, lovers - are things we all go through. That's why we're happy to revisit
Minneapolis and the WJM news room again and again. The Mary Tyler
Moore Show is the classiest of classics.

DRAGNET

Is it a riveting crime drama? Is it minimalist art? Is it the most straight-
shooting kitsch ever made? However you describe it, one thing is indis-
putably clear. Dragnet is a classic that has kept audiences glued to
their sets for decades. Maybe it's the hypnotic Dum-de-dum-dum in the
theme. Maybe it's Jack Webb's unshakeable resolve and implacable features. Or the fact that his character's name Friday reminds viewers of
the weekend. No matter, Dragnet is an arresting member of the Nick at
Nite lineup, and that's just the facts.

125

Media Kit
Nick at Nite

Designers
Michelle Willems
Mark Malabrigo

© *Nick at Nite* 1992

A pun is the humorous use of a word, or of words which are formed or sounded alike but have different meanings, in such a way as to play on two or more of the possible applications *(Webster's New World Dictionary of American Language)*. Likewise a typographic pun is a word or words that are

designed to underscore or enhance the meaning, by revealing two or more possible applications. This kind of visual pun is often created through the metamorphosis of a letterform into an image or object, but often the letterform simply substitutes for another word. Bradbury Thompson was a master at assigning letters with meaning. In one of his classic compositions from the 1940s he shows a baseball player hitting a home run. By using multiple settings of the letter O (the shape of a baseball) flying out off into space Thompson punned on the sound *OOOOOOOOOOOOUT*, as he vividly shows the ball flying OUT of the ballpark. Visual puns and typographic puns are among the most frequently used playthings in the designer's repertoire. In the quest to grab attention and convey a message puns are also the most economical way to convey complexity. But the successful pun is not less difficult in the visual than in verbal language. For Mesa, a Southwestern-style restaurant in New York, the logo uses a simple Gothic typeface with each capital letter in a different color. Though

eye-catching, what really made the logo memorable was the visual pun that was created by evenly cutting the tops of the letters off, thus making the word Mesa into a mesa. As with verbal language visual puns can engage the reader/viewer in a game of discovery.

¶uns

Logo
Bewear

Designer/Illustrator
BLACKDOG Mark Fox

© *Mark Fox/BlackDog* 1993

Logo
James Taylor
Deluxe Interstate '92

Art Director/Designer
Stephanie Mauer

© *Tisbury Tours* 1992

128

Logo
AIDS

Designers
Douglas G. Harp
Susan C. Harp

© *Douglas and Susan Harp* 1989

Self-Promotional Coaster
Design that Shines

Designer/Illustrator/Letterer
Jon Valk

© Jon Valk 1993

Magazine Spread Logo
Rolling Stone

Art Director
Fred Woodward

Designer
Gail Anderson

Letterer
Dennis Ortiz-Lopez

© Wenner Media, Inc. 1989

Logo
Fred

Designer
Fred Woodward

Letterer
Bill Gregg

© Fred Woodward 1980

129

Movie Logo
Ghost

Designer
FRANKFURT GIPS BALKIND
Peter Nguyen

© Peter Nguyen 1988

Poster
AZ You Like It

Art Directors
Forrest Richardson
Valerie Richardson

Designer
Forrest Richardson

Letterers
Forrest Richardson
Neill Fox

© *Richardson or Richardson* 1988

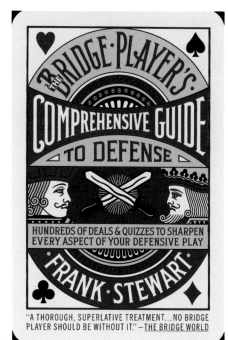

Book Cover
The New York Subway Finder

Designer/Letterer
Jon Valk

© *Stanhope Press* 1988

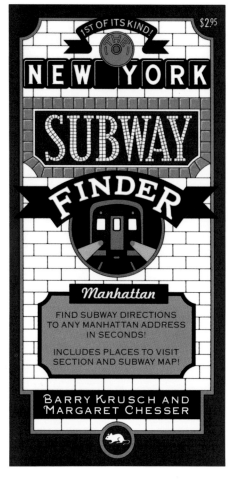

Logo
Manhattan Design

Designers
MANHATTAN DESIGN
Pat Gorman, Frank Olinsky

© *Pat Gorman & Frank Olinsky/*
Manhattan Design 1979

Book Cover
The Bridge Player's
Comprehensive
Guide to Defense

Art Director
Jackie Seow

Designer
Jon Valk

© *Fireside Books* 1990

Poster
Ambassador Arts: Letter P

Art Director
Paula Scher

Designers
Paula Scher
Ron Louie

© *Pentagram* 1993

Poster
Oz ne

Art Director/Photographer
Douglas G. Harp

Designers
Douglas G. Harp
Susan C. Harp
Linda E. Wagner

© *Douglas G. Harp* 1993

Magazine Page
Agfa Magazine

Art Director
Paula Scher

Designer
Paula Scher

© *Pentagram* 1990

Promotional Gift
Nick at Nite

Designer
Michelle Willems

© *Nick at Nite* 1993

Book Cover
The Mafia

Art Director/Designer/Illustrator
Peter Comitini

Unpublished 1992

Book Jacket
Inside the KGB
Designer
Henry Sene Yee
Illustrator
Ralph Wernli

© *Random House, Inc.* 1991

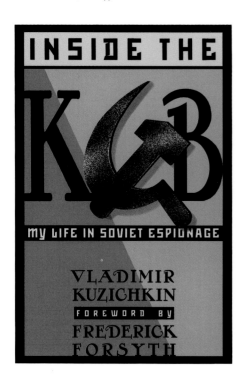

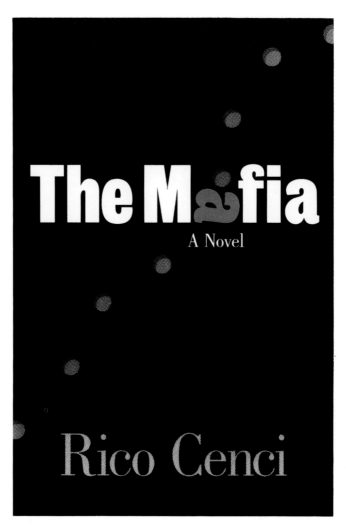

What ever happened to Mary Jo Kopechne's
five girlfriends who had the good fortune *not*
to drive off with Ted Kennedy? See page 37.
Why has there never been a best-seller or a
movie or even a television docudrama about
Chappaquiddick? See page 40. In the age of
Everythingscam **CHAPPAQUIDDICK**
and Whatevergate,
how, after 18 years, can the Chappaquiddick
cover-up remain so airtight? Good question.
And why won't anybody publish an impressive
new investigative book that for once gets a
Kennedy cousin and Chappaquiddick witness
on the record about the incident? Read this article.

EARLY IN THE MORNING
of July 19, 1969, after attending an intimate party of male political cronies and female
political aides, Senator Edward Kennedy
drove his Oldsmobile off Chappaquiddick
Island's Dyke Bridge and into Poucha Pond.
His passenger, Mary Jo Kopechne, drowned.

This is not exactly news. Most of us recall that after a con-
siderable public rumpus, Senator Kennedy took the ex-
traordinary step of going on television to explain—
altogether unconvincingly—this latest Kennedy tragedy.
Kennedy pleaded guilty to leaving the scene of an acci-
dent after causing personal injury and later promised to

*The
Unsold
Story*

BY TAD FRIEND

consider resigning his Senate seat (*Nahhh*, he evidently
decided, instead going on to win reelection three times).
After receiving a two-month suspended sentence, he
clammed up. And so did everyone else in a position to fill in
some of the blanks—the five women at the party who did not
drown in Ted Kennedy's car, the five men at the party who
did not swim away from a submerged Oldsmobile and then
lie about it. So the inquiries have blundered along without
Kennedy's help, or the help of his loyal friends at the party.
And so, naturally, strange Chappaquiddick theories
abound: Kennedy was driving; Kennedy wasn't driving;
Kennedy murdered Kopechne because she was pregnant
with his child, and jumped out of the moving car in the
nick of time; and so on.
What is news—er should be—is that Joe Gargan, a cousin
of Kennedy's who spent much of that fatal evening with the
senator, finally did unburden himself of his Chappaquid-

Magazine Spread
Spy

Art Director/Designer
Alexander Isley

© *Spy* 1987

"This is as far as I go," choked the pilot.

"Any closer, we're gonna be marshmallows at a campfire."

Maybe he was right, but I simply had to have the shot.

"Another fifty feet," I replied, the hot sulfur fumes burning my eyes as I squinted through the camera.

"Get me down fifty feet and we'll have it."

Suddenly, the boiling magma below us exploded, twisting us sideways and downward.

Ten yards away a fountain of lava burst into the sky, narrowly missing us as I scrambled to re-focus.

We seemed to be out of control, spinning wildly the fiery maw of certain death.

Next to me, the pilot frantically whistled through his teeth Hail Marys.

I whispered to my...

Poster
Science Museum of
Minnesota

Designer
Sue Crolick

© *Sue Crolick Advertising and
Design* 1991

Stationery
Joan Ostrin

Designer
Sue Crolick

© *Sue Crolick Advertising and
Design* 1990

133

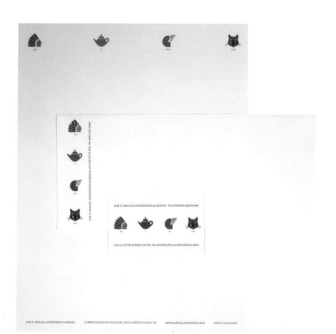

Stationery
Sue Crolick

Designer
Sue Crolick

© *Sue Crolick Advertising and
Design* 1982

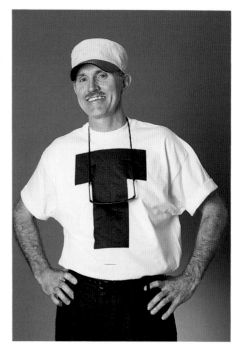

Invitation
HELL-O & Happy Holidays

Designer
Vincent Sainato

© Spot Design 1992

T-Shirts
Formal-i-T
Casual-T

Designer
Jack Summerford

© Summerford Design, Inc. 1993

Magazine Cover
Newsweek

Art Director/Designer
Peter Comitini

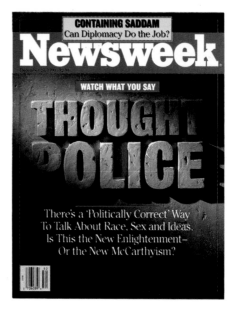

Summerford Design, Inc.
Summerford Design, Inc.
Summerford Design, Inc.
Summerford Design, Inc.
Summerford Design, Inc.
2706 Fairmount
Dallas 75201
214 748 4638
Jack

Logo
Summerford Design, Inc.

Designer
Jack Summerford

© *Jack Summerford* 1991

Record & CD Packages
Forestry

Art Directors
David Byrne
Robin Lynch

Designer
Robin Lynch

© *Sire Records* 1991

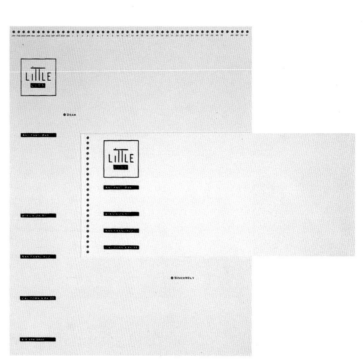

135

Stationery
Little City

Designer
Bruce Yelaska

© *Bruce Yelaska* 1987

"*There are no weird stories about rats,*" George Laws said. And then he told some. We sat at the edge of the teeming ratopolis in a basement where the city's rathunters unwind after a day going into holes with rats. The air was choked with smoke, music and the legend of that four-legged shadow of man. If rat stories did not seem weird to Laws, a foreman of exterminators for the city of New York, it was because nothing rats do surprises him. If the stories seemed weird to me, it was because I had just started collecting them. Not the commonplace assertions: that for every one of us there is one, or two, or four of them (perhaps 30 million rats in the city of New York?), or that they can squeeze through holes the size of a quarter, or that they pop up in toilets. Old news. The idea was to view the range of human experience involving rats, to dip a bucket into that polluted river! "Plastic means to a rat like a rattle to a baby," said Laws. "Any hole a rat can put his head through, he can put his body through." "They don't have no bone, just BY PHILIP WEISS gristle," said someone else. This was a rat myth. "The head's the only bone. She'll cut a hole for her head and cut it no wider and pull the rest of her body through." "Like a liquid?" "Not liquid. I wouldn't use that word." "You can put down bait from now till doomsday, you'll never kill them all." "How's that stuff work?" "His own blood drowns him. See him moving slowly, trembling just like a person having a heart attack." "Eat chicken like we eat chicken, eat bacon just like we eat bacon." "Man has been living wrong as far as sanitation is con-

Magazine Spread
Spy

Art Director
Alexander Isley

Designer
Catherine Gilmore-Barnes

© *Spy* 1988

MESA
GRILL

Logo
Mesa Grill

Art Director
Alexander Isley

Designer
Alexander Knowlton

© *Mesa Grill* 1990

Promotional Template
Isley Architects
Place and Trace

Designer
Alexander Isley

© *Isley Architects Inc.* 1986

Logo
American Museum of
the Moving Image

Designer
Alexander Isley

Illustrator
Kam Mak

© *Alexander Isley* 1991

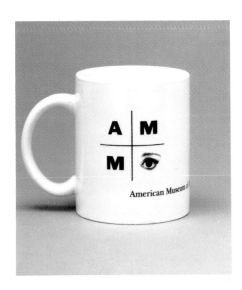

GEOGRAPHIES
of the NIGHT

NEW YORK

WESTERN CIVILIZATION

MAMBO,

BOOGALOO &

SALSA

The coming of *salsa* was revealed to me at three A.M. in Latin New York, early spring, 1960. Several Puerto Rican musicians, having played *mambos, guarachas,* and *boleros* all night at the Palladium Ballroom at Broadway and 53rd, were relaxing over coffee and jukebox Cuban music, in a small cafe on Sixth Avenue. I went up to one of them, Gilbert Lopez, the pianist in Tito

ROBERT FARRIS THOMPSON

New Music 30 *America*

I am not a choreographer; I am a choreographer/composer. The majority of choreographers will take a piece of music composed by someone else and make it visual. They get almost everything from the composer: ambiance, length of time, rhythmic structure, phrasing....In my best work I work only with myself. As a choreographer/composer I begin with rhythmic structure, the connection between dance and music. I'm very involved in the physics of sound and motion. When choreographers and composers take thought patterns and turn them

GYM.

New Music 6 *America*

Dance

·BY· LAURA DEAN·

Journal
BAM New Music America

Art Director
Alexander Isley

Designer
Alexander Knowlton

© *Brooklyn Academy of Music* 1988

137

In the 1980s the term vernacular, referring to a common language, was adopted by graphic designers who, in rejecting the slick professionalism of commercial Modernism borrowed, reappropriated, and celebrated the "dirty design" typical of the anonymous commercial artist. In a culture that is dominated by commerce, certain standards—easy, non-threatening design clichés—have developed over time to help identify and sell products. Such approaches were dubbed non-design by Modern professionals. But with the advent of the Post-Modern professional such artlessness has become a virtue, and the basis for new purposefully naïf design. In this context one could call indigenous the work of the typical sign painter. Craftspeople have been heroicized as "street artists." However, in addition to commercial street art, there is also a subcultural street art that is at odds with it. Graffiti is the principal street expression. It is illegally rendered, usually in public view on private surfaces. Graffiti has always been a personal mark. "Killroy Was Here," perhaps the world's most famous graffito, was a way for an otherwise anonymous individual to make a mark. Today graffiti is also a cultural manifestation of the disenfranchised, people who want to speak out (if only to speak at all) but do not have the official means of address. Graffiti is the ultimate vernacular, yet it is expressed in various styles and mannerisms. For despite the deliberate anonymity of its creators, graffiti is very much about publicizing oneself. It is curious, but not altogether surprising that graffiti in its variegated forms became yet another plaything for the professional designer. Scavenging from the street became a form of play, and then what was scavenged was combined with more formal design elements. Eventually vernacular became a marketable style, rather than a reflection of real cultural diversity.

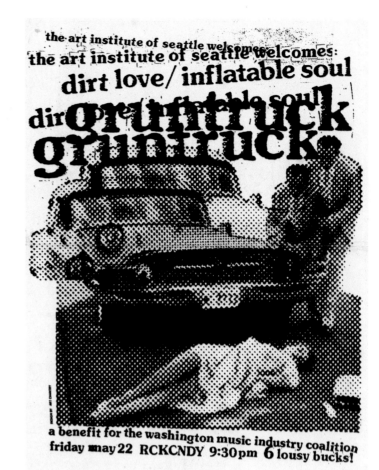

Poster
Mudhoney

Designer
Art Chantry

© *Art Chantry* 1991

Poster
Gruntruck

Designer
Art Chantry

© *Art Chantry* 1991

CD
Eat Your Heart Out

Art Directors
Jane Gulick
David Scharff

Designer
TWELVE POINT RULE

Record Company
Matador Records

© *TVT Music* 1993

Poster
Coca 1991 Season

Designer
Art Chantry

© *Art Chantry* 1991

CD Package
You're Always Welcome

Designer
Art Chantry

© *Art Chantry/Lucky Records* 1993

LIVE IN THE BUCKLE OF THE BIBLE BELT
FREE ADMISSION   FREE ADMISSION
CREATIVE (REVIVAL) CRUSADE
PORTFOLIO CENTER
ASSEMBLY HALL
125 BENNETT ST., ATLANTA, GEORGIA
THURS., SEPT. 23, 1993
YOUR DEVOTED FOLLOWERS AWAIT THE TRAIN TO THE PROMISED LAND

2:00 P.M. - READ THE GOOD BOOKS
4:00 - 6:00 P.M. - MEET THEIR MAKERS
8:00 P.M. - FINAL BLESSING OF GRADUATES
COME EXPECTING A MIRACLE AND LEAVE WITH A CHOSEN FEW
SEE THE LIGHT!   SEE THE BOOKS!

TO WITNESS, CALL
CAROL VICK AT 1-800-255-3169

Creative: Two Drink Minimum (C.W. Susan Treacy; A.D. Todd Gallentine)   Typesetting and Printing: Southern Poster

Poster
Creative Revival

Creative Director
Roger Richards

Art Director
Todd Gallentine

Typesetting
Southern Poster

© *Portfolio Center* 1992

142

CD/Package
Ain't No Other

Art Director
Lynn Kowalewski

Photographer
Merlyn Rosenberg

© *Atlantic Recording Corp./
First Priority Music* 1993

Tabloid Cover
Northwest Extra!

Designer
Art Chantry

Illustrator
Robert Crumb

© *Art Chantry* 1989

Poster
New City Theater

Designer
Art Chantry

© *Art Chantry* 1990

Poster
Czechoslovakian Printmakers

Designer
Art Chantry

© *Art Chantry* 1989

Logos
Bark Promo Cards

Designers
SMOKEBOMB STUDIO
Nancy Mazzei, Brian Kelly

© *Smokebomb Studio* 1992

Poster
Cramps

Designer/Illustrator
Philip Cooper

© *ArtRock–San Francisco, CA* 1989

CD Package
Taurus No Bull

Designers
SMOKEBOMB STUDIO
Nancy Mazzei, Brian Kelly

© *TVT Records* 1993

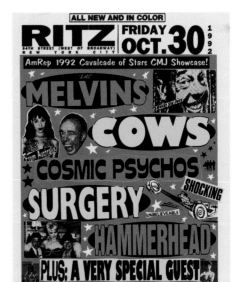

Poster
AmRep 1992 CMJ Showcase

Designer
Frank Kozik

© *Frank Kozik c/o ArtRock–
San Francisco, CA* 1992

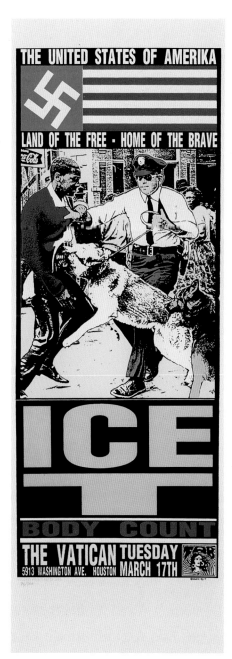

Poster
Sub Pop Ultra Lame Fest
Designer
ARTROCK Frank Kozik

© *Frank Kozik c/o ArtRock-*
San Francisco, CA 1992

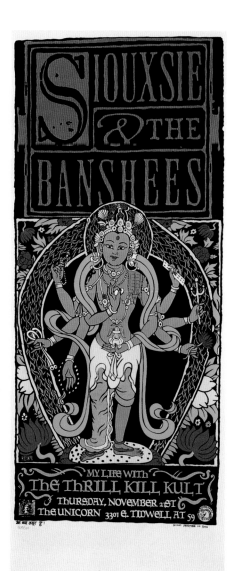

145

Poster
Ice T
Designer
ARTROCK Frank Kozik

© *Frank Kozik c/o ArtRock-*
San Francisco, CA 1992

Poster
Siouxsie and the Banshees
Designer
ARTROCK Frank Kozik

© *Frank Kozik c/o ArtRock-*
San Francisco, CA 1991

► RHYMES FOR MODERN TIMES

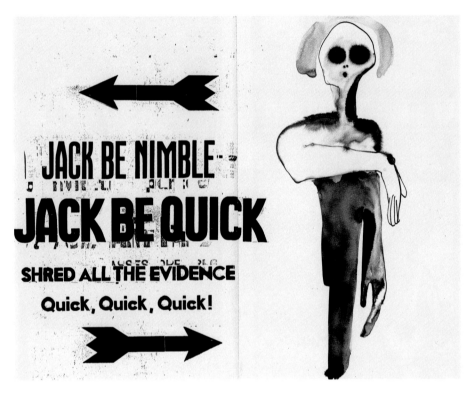

← JACK BE NIMBLE ·
JACK BE QUICK
SHRED ALL THE EVIDENCE
Quick, Quick, Quick!
→

AS I WAS COMING DOWN THE STAIR

I MET A MAN WHO WASN'T THERE.

HE WAVED A PAPER CUP AT ME $$

WHICH I WAS ABLE NOT TO SEE.

HE WASN'T THERE AGAIN TODAY

I WISH THAT MAN WOULD GO AWAY!

Book Spreads
Mordant Rhymes for Modern Times

Designer
Yolanda Cuomo

Illustrator
Fran Bull

Woodtype Handsetter
Gwynne Truglio

© Fran Bull 1990

THIS IS THE HOUSE THAT
CRACK BUILT

This is the drug
That lay in the house that Crack built.

This is the rat who sold the drug
That lay in the house that Crack built.

This is the cat who needed the shot
And bought from the rat
Who sold the drug
That lay in the house that Crack built.

This is the cop who worried the cat
Who needed the shot
And bought from the rat
Who sold the drug
That lay in the house that Crack built.

This is the man all tattered and torn
Who shot the cop who worried the cat
Who needed the shot
And bought from the rat who sold the drug
That lay in the house that Crack built.

This is the maiden all forlorn
Who carries a baby yet unborn
By the tattered man who killed the cop
Who worried the cat
Who needed the shot
And bought from the rat who sold the drug
That lay in the house that Crack built.

Logo
Tad

Designer
Art Chantry

© *Art Chantry* 1991

FULGHUM HEAVY INDUSTRIES

147

Letterhead Imprint
Fulghum Heavy Industries

Designer
Art Chantry

© *Art Chantry* 1990

Logo
Artists' Products

Designer
Art Chantry

© *Art Chantry* 1989

Chapter 14

T he face is the most expressive of our dramatic and comedic tools, and making silly faces is a fundamental part of the play instinct. Likewise making faces from letterforms is key to contemporary typeplay. A type face is the ultimate pun since all the letters serve other functions. However, within the typeface *discipline* numerous approaches are practiced. Among them, type used simply as line or shape (i.e. Os for eyes, T for nose, G for ears, and Xs for hair), or metamorphosed into a face (i.e. a G, Q, or O is used as

the outline of a head, or an R, B, or H are the body), or as a pure pun (i.e. the letters that make up the face or body can also be read as a word or phrase). Typeface design can be as easy as children's art, or as complex as a Cubist collage. Regardless, the aim is to have fun with, indeed tweak the senses of the viewer. Type faces are not appropriate for all design problems, but given their frequency in design annuals and shows, the face is certainly one of the most popular typographic toys on the market.

148

Book Jacket
Uncommon Wisdom

Art Director/Designer
Paula Scher

© *Pentagram* 1988

Magazine Page
Rolling Stone

Art Director
Fred Woodward

Designer
Debra Bishop

Letterer
Anita Karl

© *Wenner Media, Inc.* 1991

Brochure
Type That Talks

Designers
Jeff Fabian
Sam Shelton
Jean Kane

© *KINETIK* 1989

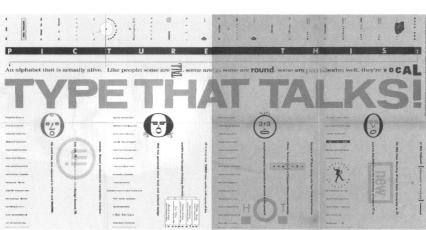

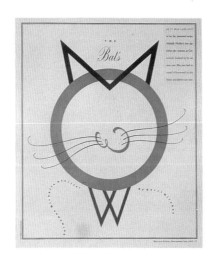

Magazine Page
Rolling Stone

Art Director/Designer
Fred Woodward

Letterer
Anita Karl

© *Wenner Media, Inc.* 1992

Poster
Moving Announcement

Art Directors
Takaaki Matsumoto
Michael McGinn

Designer
Takaaki Matsumoto

© *M Plus M, Incorporated* 1989

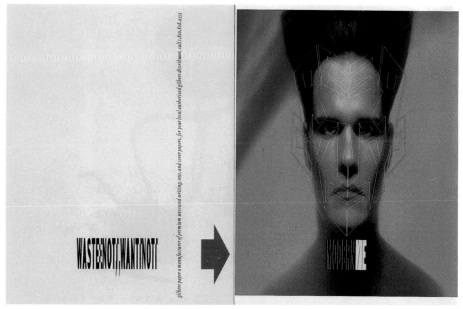

Advertisement
Gilbert Paper

Designer
THIRST Rick Valicenti

© *THIRST* 1992

151

Postcard
Our Vacation '92

Designer
Randy Tibbott

Illustrator
Natasha Lessnik

© *Our Designs, Inc.* 1992

152

Invitation
AIGA Communication
Graphics Announcement

Designer
Alexander Isley

© *Alexander Isley* 1988

Postcard
Our New Year's Greeting '93

Art Director
Randy Tibbott

Designer
Natasha Lessnik

© *Our Designs, Inc.* 1993

Annual Report Logo
Dallas Zoological Society

Designer
Scott Ray

© *Peterson & Company* 1990

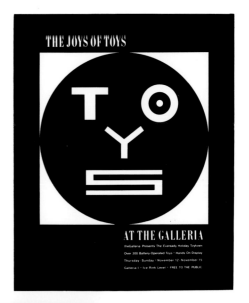

Poster
Toys

Creative Director
THE HILL GROUP Chris Hill

Designer
David Lerch

© *The Hill Group* 1987

153

Poster
Zoot Restaurant

Designer
Lana Rigsby

© *Rigsby Design* 1991

Poster
Öola

Art Director
Paula Scher

Designers
Paula Scher
Debra Bishop

© *Pentagram* 1990

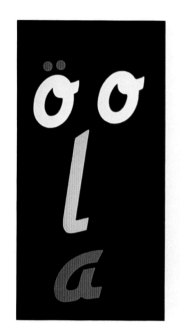

Magazine Spread
May Typography Quarterly

Designer
Sue Crolick

© *Sue Crolick Advertising and Design* 1990

154

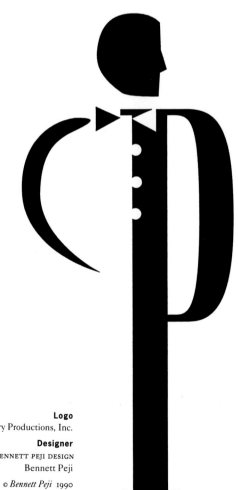

Logo
Culinary Productions, Inc.

Designer
BENNETT PEJI DESIGN
Bennett Peji

© *Bennett Peji* 1990

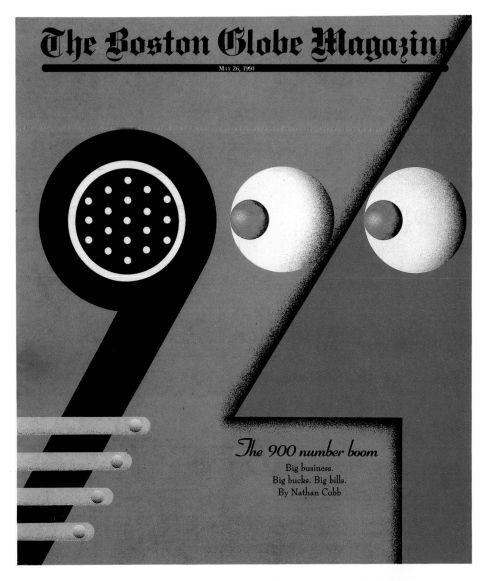

Magazine Cover
The Boston Globe Magazine

Designers
Terry Allen
Lucy Bartholomay

Illustrator
Terry Allen

Typography
Lucy Bartholomay

© *The Boston Globe*
Newspaper Co. 1991

**Promotional Book
Cover/Spread**
Richard Solomon

Art Director/Designer
Louise Fili

© *Richard Solomon* 1992

Logo
JCH TeleGraphics

Art Directors
Takaaki Matsumoto
Michael McGinn

Designer
Michael McGinn

© *M Plus M, Incorporated* 1988

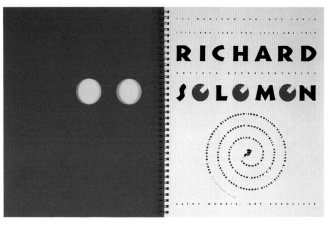

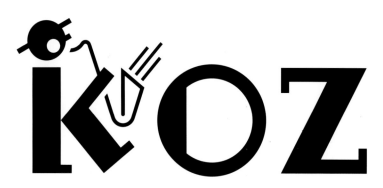

Logo
Embarko

Designer/Illustrator/Letterer
BLACKDOG Mark Fox

© Mark Fox/BlackDog 1989

Logo
Dave Koz

Art Directors
Tommy Steele
Jeff Fey

Designer/Illustrator
BLACKDOG Mark Fox

© Mark Fox/BlackDog 1990

Tales of a Revealing Nature

Rita Rudner

Naked Beneath My Clothes

Book Cover
Naked Beneath My Clothes

Art Director
Michael Ian Kaye

Designer
Robert Clyde Anderson

Photographer
Kenneth Bank

© Viking Penguin 1993

Book Cover
Inside the KGB
Designer/Illustrator
Peter Comitini
Unpublished 1992

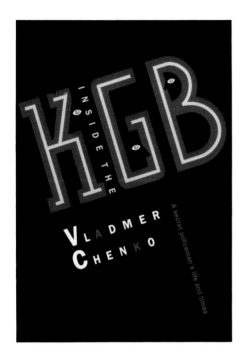

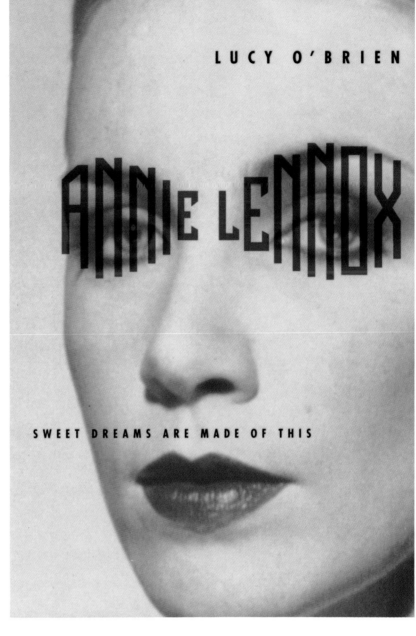

LUCY O'BRIEN

SWEET DREAMS ARE MADE OF THIS

157

On-Air Logos
MTV Ears
MTV Eyeball
Designer
Pat Gorman
© *Pat Gorman (MTV)* 1989

Book Cover
Annie Lennox
Art Director
Henry Sene Yee
Designer
Angela Skouras
Photographer
RETNA Lewis Ziolek
© *St. Martin's Press* 1993

Contrary to the Bible, in the beginning was the image. If one is to accept theories of prehistory over those of religious doctrine, the spoken word took time to evolve and the written word did not catch on right away, either. The Lascaux caves contain the evidence of the primitive's need to express through marks that comment on the environment. One can imagine the caveperson's frustration at not being able to further amplify these visual ideas with verbal language. Despite the expressive power of the grunt, being able to

combine words into sentences and paragraphs to illustrate the picture might have pushed back the discovery of charades by millennia, but would have considerably increased the ability to effortlessly communicate. It is not surprising that after the word came and writing developed there was a primal need to embellish it with images, for words alone were not enough to communicate The Word. Manuscript illuminators of old commanded inflated hourly rates for it was commonly believed that readers needed the inducement of an image to enter into reading a text. And yet even back then there was a tension between editor and art director over the ratio of text versus image. The illuminated initial was developed as a means of combining letter and picture into a single image. The invention of type in the sixteenth century was a boon to mass communications but the death knell of complex illumination. The technology simply did not allow for the total integration of letter and picture. During the sixteenth century, advances in typography further eroded this relationship.

The separation of illustration and ornament from type was common until the nineteenth century, when artists of the Art Nouveau movement and the poster revolution of the Belle Epoch wed hand-drawn letters with art. Shortly after, the Aesthetic and Arts and Crafts movements reprised certain Medieval styles of integrated type and image. And yet despite these historical roots the total integration of type and image is a Modern invention. Advanced printing technology and reverence for machine-made art made it possible to join the two elements into one composition. The marriage of type and image is the cornerstone of graphic design, and nothing can tear it asunder.

TYPE
&

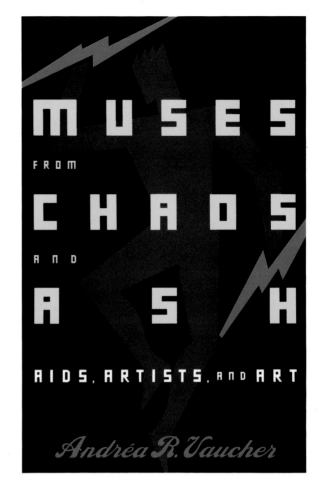

Book Jacket
Muses from Chaos and Ash

Art Director
Krystyna Skalski

Designer
Carin Goldberg

© *Grove Press* 1992

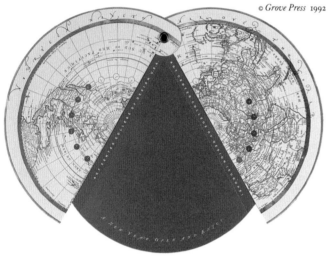

Greeting Card
New Year Greeting

Designer
Rebeca Mendez

© *Art Center College of Design* 1989

Magazine Cover
Time

Art Director/Designer
Mirko Ilic

© *Time Warner Inc.* 1991

Poster
Bathhouse Theatre
Designer
Art Chantry
© *Art Chantry* 1983

Magazine Cover
Emigre
Art Director/Designer
Rudy Vanderlans
© *Emigre* 1992

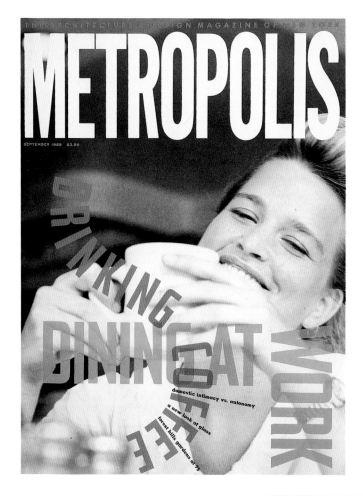

Magazine Cover
Metropolis

Art Director/Designer
Helene Silverman

Photographer
Kristine Larsen

© *Metropolis* 1988

Logos
Byron Priess Multimedia

Art Director
Paula Scher

Designers
Paula Scher
Ron Louie

162   © *Pentagram* 1993

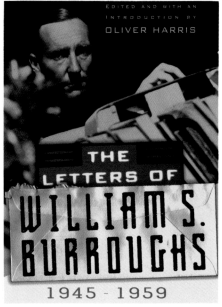

Book Jacket
The Letters of
William S. Burroughs

Designer
Paul Buckley

Photographer
Allen Ginsbergh

© *Penguin USA* 1993

Record Sleeve
Fast Piss Blues/I Got the Blues

Art Director/Letterer
Robert Hamilton

Illustrator
Roderigo Avila

© *Matador Records* 1992

Poster
Greenleaf Medical

Art Director/Designer/Letterer
Earl Gee

Photographer
Geoffrey Nelson

© *Earl Gee Design* 1990

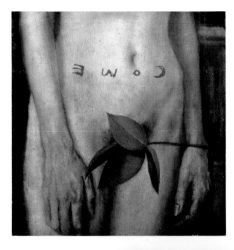

Poster
December Calendar

Art Director
Lisa Levin

Designer
Ashlie Benton

© *Lisa Levin* 1992

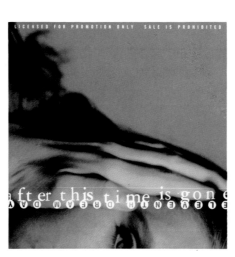

Book Jacket
Olga: Revolutionary and Martyr

Art Director
Krystyna Skalski

Designer
Carin Goldberg

© *Grove Press* 1989

Magazine Page
Rolling Stone

Art Director
Fred Woodward

Designer
Debra Bishop

Photographer
Doug Rosa

© *Wenner Media, Inc.* 1993

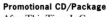

Promotional CD/Package
After This Time Is Gone

Art Director
Melanie Nissen

Designer
Frank Gargiulo

Photographer
Amy Guip

© *Atlantic Recording Corp.* 1993

Book Jacket
A Good Scent from a
Strange Mountain

Art Directors
Krystyna Skalski
Raquel Jaramillo

Designer
Carin Goldberg

Illustrator
Neil Flewellen

© *Henry Holt* 1992

Book Jacket
A Visit Home

Art Director
Frank Metz

Designer
Carin Goldberg

Photographer
Barry Marcus

© *Simon & Schuster* 1993

Book Jacket
The Great German Films

Designer
Louise Fili

© *Louise Fili* 1991

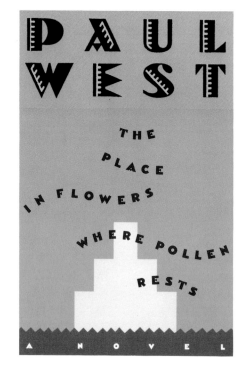

Book Jacket
The Place in Flowers
Where Pollen Rests

Art Director
Alex Gotfryd

Designer
Carin Goldberg

© *Doubleday* 1988

Book Jacket
This Day and Age

Designer
Archie Ferguson

Photographer
Diana Klein

© *Alfred A. Knopf* 1992

166

Book Jacket
Hole in the Sky

Art Director
Carol Devine Carson

Designer
Barbara de Wilde

Photographer
Kurt Marcus

© *Alfred A. Knopf* 1992

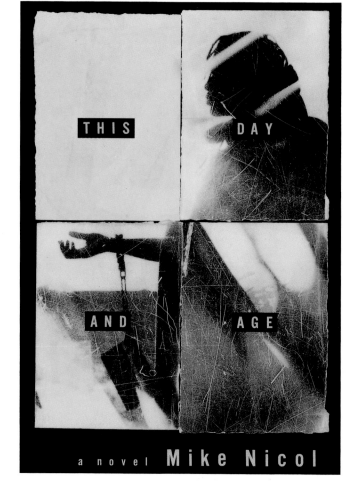

Book Jacket
Elton John: The Biography

Art Director
John Fontana

Designer
Henry Sene Yee

Photographers
LONDON FEATURES INT'L.
P. Ollern Shaw
Katherine Mc Gylnn *still life*

© *Harmony Books, a division of*
Crown Publishers, Inc. 1992

Book Jacket
Motor City

Designer
Archie Ferguson

© *Alfred A. Knopf* 1992

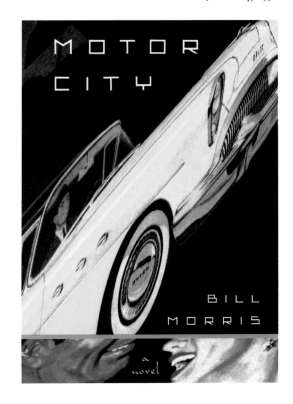

Book Jacket
A Poet's Bible

Art Director
Victor Weaver

Designer
Carin Goldberg

Illustrator
Melanie Marder Parks

© *Hyperion Books* 1992

Invitation Booklet
Tuna and Pat's Wedding

Art Director
Pat Gorman

Illustrator
Lynda Barry

© *Pat Gorman* 1989

Book Cover
Head Comix

Art Director
Stacey Holston

Designer/Illustrator
R. Crumb

© *R. Crumb* 1987

Album Cover
Big World

Designer
ROSENWORLD Laurie Rosenwald

Illustrator
Serge Clerc

© *A&M Records* 1986

Book Cover
Bring the Noise

Art Director
John Fontana

Designer/Letterer
Henry Sene Yee

© *Harmony Books, a division of Crown Publishers, Inc.* 1991

169

Album Cover
Free South Africa

Designer
Art Chantry

© *Art Chantry/Out Front Music* 1990

Brochure
CLaGS

Designer
Chip Kidd

© *Chip Kidd* 1988

Brochure
Stat Store Capabilities

Art Director/Designer
Alexander Isley

© *Stat Store* 1988

Book Jacket
Fish Boy

Designers
Chip Kidd
Barbara de Wilde

© *Chip Kidd and Barbara de Wilde* 1991

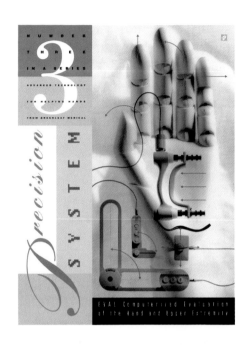

Ad Series
Greenleaf Medical

Art Director/Designer/Letterer
Earl Gee

Photographer
Geoffrey Nelson

© *Earl Gee Design* 1992

Chapter 16

The invention of the typewriter in the late nineteenth century was as revolutionary as that of the personal computer in the late twentieth and posed many of the same challenges. In addition to conceiving and manufacturing a mechanism for this remarkable writing machine, the question of what letterforms it should include had to have been a major issue. The decision to use the two slab serif faces (pica and elite) defined the look of business communications for over a century. Although variations on the form were designed over time, the basic appearance of a typewritten page did not significantly change—even after IBM introduced its replaceable golf ball with numerous other typestyles—until the advent of the word processor. Typewriter type became forever associated with personal or business writing, while type foundry faces were, of course, the exclusive province of professional printing. The distinction was so ingrained that, although American Typefoundry offered *American Typewriter* as a hot metal cut in various sizes and weights, it was only used professionally when a typographer wanted to evoke informal formality. Commercial artists preferred the standard types to typewriter because the latter did not command authority on the printed page. And yet certain Modern designers from the 1930s found in actual typewriter type the same kind of naively expressive quality that early Macintosh typographers found in low resolution dot matrix type. Among the masters of the Modern, Alexey Brodovitch and Paul Rand produced seminal compositions that used typewriter type to express their rebellion against traditional typography. After they opened the gates, typewriter became a very common way for designers to express immediacy. Today with thousands of fonts available to the average secretary, more formal faces are being used instead of typewriter type. Probably in time this ubiquitously popular face will become as anachronistic as Old English or Fraktur, but it will always be the most democratic of the world's faces.

TXXYPE -

WRITER

TYPE

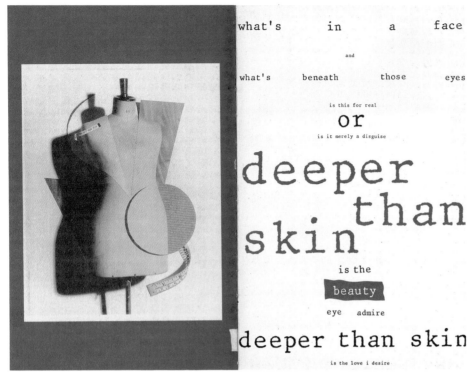

what's   in   a   face

and

what's   beneath   those   eyes

is this for real

or

is it merely a disguise

deeper
than
skin

is the

beauty

eye   admire

deeper than skin

is the love i desire

Invitation
DIFFA

Designers
Jeff Fabian
Laura Latham
Sam Shelton

Photographer
Geof Kern

© *DIFFA DC* 1991

something wonder
ful happens ◼silent
auction throughout
the evening ◼6:30pm
dinner guests arrive
◼9pm party guests ar
rive ◼10pm fashion
show ◼11pm dancing◼

174

Logo
VH-1 Classic Rock

Designer
SMOKEBOMB STUDIO Nancy Mazzei

© *VH-1* 1991

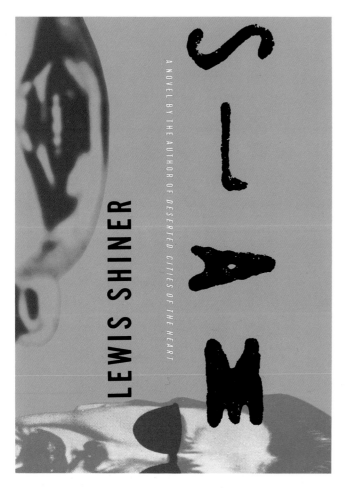

Book Jacket
Slam
Designer
Chip Kidd
© *Chip Kidd* 1990

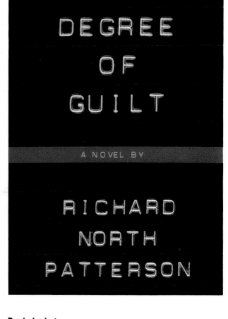

Book Jacket
Degree of Guilt
Art Director/Designer
Carol Devine Carson
© *Alfred A. Knopf* 1993

175

Book Cover
Edge City
Designer
Paul Buckley
© *Penguin USA* 1993

Magazine Cover
Rolling Stone

Art Director/Designer
Fred Woodward

Photographer
Herb Ritts

© *Wenner Media, Inc.* 1992

Book Jacket
Breaking Blue

Designer
Barbara de Wilde

Photographer
Geoff Spear

© *Barbara de Wilde* 1991

Book Jacket
Life Sketches

Designer
Archie Ferguson

© *Alfred A. Knopf* 1989

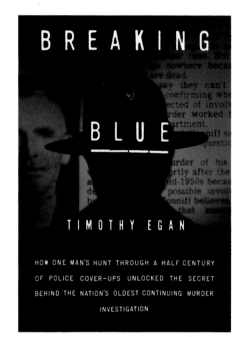

176

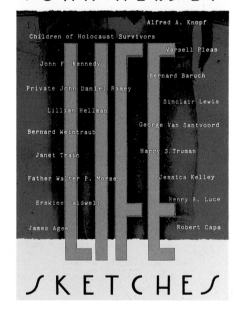

Magazine Spread
Rolling Stone

Art Director
Fred Woodward

Designer
Angela Skouras

Illustrator
Everett Peck

© *Wenner Media, Inc.* 1992

Poster
Low Technology

Designer
Art Chantry

© *Art Chantry* 1989

Book Cover
No Mercy

Designer
Frank Gargiulo

Photographer
Jerald Frampton

© *Atlantic Monthly Press* 1989

Typeface Specimen
Back Spacer

Designer
SMOKEBOMB STUDIO
Nancy Mazzei, Brian Kelly

© *Smokebomb Studio* 1993

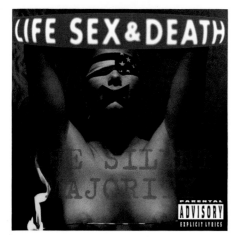

CD Package
The Silent Majority

Designers
P. Scott Makela
Debora Norcross

Photographer
Amy Guip

© *Warner Bros. Records* 1992

Book Cover
Great Jones Street

Designer
Michael Ian Kaye

Photographer
Ralph Gibson

© *Penguin* 1994

Chapter 17

Typography serves the word, and the word communicates ideas. After all the typeplay, after all the transcendent notions of graphic design as art, in the final analysis type is an instrument of meaning, and typography is its structural manifestation. However, in the end the arrangement is irrelevant—centered, flush left, flush right, symmetrical or asymmetrical, are choices that contribute to the aesthetics of a design. Rather what is important is how clearly the word, and ultimately the message, is

presented. But even this is debatable. Classical humanist typography is devoted to making words accessible. Post-Modern deconstructivist typography is concerned with making words emote. What is more important, and to whom? Should everyone read the same words in the same way, or should room be set aside for ambiguity and nuance? This is the most significant question concerning typography today. In the final analysis style is no more or less than an accent. The world is comprised of countless languages, so why should typography be limited to a few accents? The Modern's mission to universalize language was not all that different from the Church's mission to convert the heathens—and rid them of their cultural difference. Cultures have their own beliefs, ethics, rituals, and languages. But even in most primitive or ancient languages there are equivalent words (or signs) in other languages. While the curse of Babel—the plethora of languages—might seem counterproductive in terms of

global intercourse, in fact each language contributes to the worldview. Likewise typography need not be constricted by the neutrality imposed by some global idealism. What is key to effective typography is not that strict rules are obeyed, or for that matter, challenged, but that meaning is conveyed effectively. In this sense it is important to address the basics, the fundamental concern of language and its servants. Exploring how the word alone is communicated is the most basic issue in typography.